Quick
wards
2002

PRESS

147

VOGUE
fashion awards
FRIDAY THE 20TH
Live - Theater at Madison Square Garden
October 2000

CREW

BRITISH ACADEMY
FILM AWARDS

press conference
mezz 1

2005

orange

Blackball World Premiere

SPECIAL
ACCESS

PHOTOGRAPHERS

HOGAN, Dave

THE SUN

Photographer

D1397003

MTV VMA.c
video_music_awards

FROM THE DIRECTOR OF
'TROY' and 'THE PERFECT STORM'

POSEIDON

2003

SKIN TWO RUBBER
BALL WEEKEND
OCTOBER 3-6 2003

Valid for:
TG Rubber Ball Special 3/10
House of Flesh 4/10
Expo Sat 4/10
Expo Sun 5/10
Rubber Ball 6/10
VIP After Party 6/10

NAME:
DAVE HOGAN

SKIN TWO PHOTO

PATHÉ!

RESIDENT
EVIL

ROLLING
STONES
EURO 07

PHOTOGRAPHE

PRESS

015

MEDIA
tlantic launch day

e

2001
WORLD MUSIC AWARDS
le sporting

PRESS

Name HOGAN

europe*m

2003
STOCKHOLM

grapher

Alfie

RLD MUSIC AWARDS
8th MAY 1996

CE

OGAN Dave
THE SUN
UK

RETURN OF THE

SPICE
GIRLS

Monte-Carlo Sporting Club
girls.com

RED CARPET
ONLY

SS

rv To Venue

SONY

Capital Gold

LEGENDS
Awards

26TH SEPTEMBER 2003

PRESS

birthday girl.

Tuesday 25th June 2002

BRITISH
ACADEMY
TELEVISION
AWARDS

Pioneer

7th May 2006
itv Productions

ELTON JOHN
TOUR 2000

Madison Square Garden

ACCESS

BRIT
AWARDS

MON 14 FEB 1994
SPONSORED BY
BRITANNIA MUSIC CLUB B

MAY 18, 199
1st Annual
Music Indus
Tennis Ope

The Racquet Ce
Studio City

EDINBURGH 50,000
FINAL PUSH. JULY 6. 200

LONG WALK TO JUSTICE

PRESS PASS

RESS/MEDIA
TEAM AAA

WARNER
VILLAGE

FILM FOUR 4

Variety Club

PARK ROOM

The British Academy Award is based on design by

MEDIA

OINK SCREENERS

I would like to dedicate this book to my dear Mum, who left us very suddenly this summer. I'm still struggling to cope with her loss. You don't realise how much you miss your Mum until she's gone, so tell your Mum you love her today.

This edition first published in the UK in 2008
By Green Umbrella Publishing

© Green Umbrella Publishing 2008

www.gupublishing.co.uk

Publishers: Jules Gammond and Vanessa Gardner

Creative Director: Kevin Gardner

The right of Dave Hogan & David Clayton to be identified as authors of this book have been asserted by him in accordance with the Copyright, Designs and Patents Act 1988.

Printed and bound in Italy

ISBN: 978-1-906229-97-9

Foreword by
**Gordon
Smart**
THE SUN'S
Bizarre Column Editor

ACCESS
ALL
AREAS

Behind the scenes with THE SUN'S Celebrity photographer
Dave Hogan

Green**Umbrella**
Publishing

ACCESS
ALL
AREAS

Contents

Foreword 6

Introduction 8

Madonna 14

Simon Cowell 20

Louis Walsh 22

Take That 24

Robbie Williams 28

Boybands 32

Michael Jackson 34

The Spice Girls 38

Posh & Becks 42

Britney Spears 44

Christina Aguilera 46

Paul McCartney 48

The Krays 52

Planet Hollywood 54

Oasis 56

James Bond 60

Chris Moyles 64

Best of the Caners 66

Live Aid & Sir Bob 68

Band Aid 2 76

Live 8 78

Diana 82

Contents

46664	84	**Rod Stewart**	130
Mandela	88	**Mariah Carey**	132
Bono & U2	90	**Duran Duran**	136
Boy George	94	**The Brits**	138
The Rolling Stones	96	**Natasha Bedingfield**	144
Elton John	106	**Gorgeous Girls**	146
Prince	110	**Little Britain**	148
Rock & Pop Legends	112	**Coldplay**	150
Screen Icons	118	**Upcoming Talent**	152
The Osbournes	120	**Gordon Brown**	154
Girls Aloud	124	**The Editors**	156
Kylie	126		

Contents

Foreword
By Gordon Smart

Few people in the world can claim to have been run over and survived. There are even fewer in the world that have been run over by Madonna and lived to tell the tale. In fact, there is only one man who didn't just live to recount the story – he has lived to take the photographs too.

Characters like Dave Hogan, The Sun's veteran showbiz photographer, are few and far between. A much-loved celebrity snapper, a showbiz encyclopaedia and a very useful security guard rolled into one giant 6ft 4in, burly, Welsh frame.

He has out-partied Robbie Williams. He has been thrown out of Brazil for an outrageous week-long tear-up with Tina Turner. Then there was the time he sent an insanely jealous Liam Gallagher's blood pressure through the roof by faxing cheeky messages to the Manc hellraiser's house in London as he larked around with a bikini-clad Patsy Kensit on a yacht in the Bahamas.

I feel lucky to work with Hogie. Having a man of experience by your side in a showbiz interview is like starting a football match 1-0 up. Without fail he has met and photographed whoever you are going to see at least once before. They all remember him too.

Take the Spice Girls reunion press conference at the O2 Arena last year for example. The world's media were waiting for Posh, Scary, Baby, Ginger and Sporty to emerge for the first time together as a band for six years. A sea of flashbulbs were poised to pop as Girl Power re-emerged for a final swansong.

After the girls had tottered out and the cameras settled briefly for questions I could see and hear an almighty scrap kicking off in the pit. Jostling for position had turned into fisticuffs – and there was only one man left standing when the commotion calmed down – Hogie. Over a thousand waiting reporters and photographers, an army of publicists and five popstars watched as a polite, but very angry giant of a snapper, made it clear he was the boss. As he slung his camera back over his shoulder the girls, one by one, said, "Hi Dave."

You just can't buy that kind of experience and presence, as Little Britain star David Walliams found out at Live 8. He said: "Dave Hogan is a delight. He is extremely friendly and courteous which is why he always gets the best shots. I remember when me and Matt were entering the backstage area at Live 8. We were there to introduce Sir Elton John and dressed as Lou and Andy. The first person we bumped into was Sir Paul McCartney, you know out of The Beatles. Dave appeared with his camera and we stayed in character as Sir Paul pretended to be caring for Andy, holding his hand and looking concerned! It was hilarious! It was all over in seconds but Dave got a really great shot that appeared in lots of newspapers the next day. I gave a copy of the shot to Matt for his birthday. It has pride of place in his study. We were so pleased Dave was there to get such a fun shot of us meeting one of our absolute idols!"

This is a man who rents his holiday home to the Prime Minister. He was the first photographer the Kray's turned to when a sinister but flattering portrait was required to be taken. He was Robbie Williams' babysitter when he left Take That and needed someone to look after him.

He does have a terrible habit of eating your bread roll on long haul flights. A small drawback in an armoury of endless attributes.

From the glamour of Butlins summer season Hogie has grafted solidly, pulling himself up by the scruff of the neck to achieve unprecedented success on Fleet Street.

I have only known Hogie for five years but it feels like 15. A string of long haul flights, a week in Cannes and endless hours waiting for that brief moment of opportunity for a quick picture with a famous face have allowed him the chance to flex his story telling skills.

I feel like I was carrying his lens for him when he was making his name taking pictures at the door of Stringfellows. I could have been on the boat with him when he soiled Patsy Kensit's yacht with the contents of his stomach (a big one at that). I almost feel like I was a passenger in the car when the Reggie Kray funeral procession took a wrong turn because Hogie was lost in East London.

The fact is, he is the only photographer I would ever want to go into battle with. Andy Coulson once said the closest he ever came to death was choking on a cocktail sausage at a showbiz party. If Hogie is there with you, the cocktail sausages have gone before the Heimlich manoeuvre is required.

Prince of Darkness Ozzy Osbourne and wife Sharon are proof of his appeal to famous faces.

Sharon said: "He is a man who knows his craft. It seems like he's always around, but he's always a pleasure to deal with.   As soon as you see Dave Hogan it just makes you smile. I always stop to give him a big hug whenever I see him."

Ozzy agreed: "We always have a good laugh. I think Hogie's one of the few who has been around longer than me!"

I once witnessed Hogie discipline Shakin' Stevens for being arrogant with a former colleague. To say he was Shakin' after suffering the wrath of his fellow Welshman would be an understatement.

I have also seen how fast his reactions are in battle when showbiz shenanigans are kicking off around him. He is the Clint Eastwood of this game. His Nikon D2 is his magnum, shooting the showbiz heroes and villains around him. The way he captured the moment Sarah Harding downed a bottle of whisky at the NME Awards in 2007 was nothing short of brilliant.

All the glowing praise is justified – every Bizarre editor before me will drink to that, as they all do so well. Not least because of his secret file of incriminating pictures he has of them all – but not me… yet.

Former Bizarre man Piers Morgan said: "I spent five years flying round the world with Hogie – interviewing, partying with, and infuriating the biggest stars.

He photographed me doing everything from dancing with Madonna in Cannes, arm-wrestling with Jean-Claude Van Damme in New York, boxing with Sly Stallone in Italy, and having a snowball fight with Don Johnson and Melanie Griffith in Aspen.

And in the end, I enjoyed it all so much that I decided to give up newspapers and become a talentless, overpaid, overrated celebrity myself.

Hogie is one of the best, and best-loved, photographers in showbusiness, and it was a pleasure to work with him."

If this book is half as good as it sounds after an argument with a stuck-up celebrity followed by a 10 hour flight and three bottles of wine, then it will be a best-seller. At the very least it should sell more than Piers' The Insider. I just hope this trend won't see Hogie judging Britain's Got Talent 2011.

The country isn't ready to acknowledge scuba diving photographers just yet.

Award winning film director and writer Richard Curtis summed Hogie up perfectly. Talking about his work on a historic summer's day back in 2005, he said: "Dave's work on Live 8 proved what a substantial and meaty photographer he really is. He captured that amazing day, in all its optimistic strangeness and total exhaustion, perfectly."

It's not just Live 8 and other historic occasions like Live Earth and Concert For Diana. Hogie has captured an endless list of celebs and a string of Bizarre editors in all our optimistic strangeness and total exhaustion over the years.

Gordon Smart, Bizarre Editor
November 2007 – Present

Foreword

Introduction
Finding Focus

I grew up in semi-rural Wales as an average kid and by my teens, I hadn't a bloody clue what I wanted to do with my life. Most of my mates joined the Army or began various apprenticeships and as a career in the military was never on my agenda, I became an apprentice draughtsman – don't ask me why because I hadn't got a clue myself – it just sort of fell in my lap and I went along with it.

I was offered an apprenticeship when the guy who was my boss said, "You don't really want to do this, do you?" I told him that I wasn't really sure what I wanted to do and he told me that his son was at Shrewsbury Art College – and having the time of his life. That last bit caught my imagination and I think he could sense as much, so he picked up the phone and called the college for me and arranged a meeting on my behalf there and then. I went along, they accepted me and I began a two-year foundation art course instead of taking steps towards becoming a draughtsman.

I settled in quickly at Shrewsbury and enjoyed the variety of coursework and the chance to immerse myself in a completely creative environment. I soon had the opportunity to photograph a nude woman and in an instant, could see the appeal of photography!

The two years passed quickly and I loved every minute of it and it was soon time to choose my career path. The choice was either a degree in ceramics or photography and you can probably guess which one I chose... yes; I went down that lucrative road of ceramics!

"I quit my degree and landed a job as resident snapper at Butlin's Holiday Camp."

I'd secured a place at the Central School of Art and Design in London and embarked on a three-year course, and with 17 girls and just three guys, I was certain I'd made the right choice. I had an absolute ball, as you might imagine, but there was something gnawing away at the back of my mind and despite being happy and enjoying myself, I knew that a career in ceramics just wasn't for me. I'd spent three months travelling around the USA before starting my degree and had enjoyed the freedom and sense of adventure during what was an eye-opening time for a naïve teenager. I had itchy feet and felt the need to travel again, so halfway through my time at Central School, I realised that it would be much easier to see the world with a camera than by sitting behind a potter's wheel. I needed a shift in direction so I began looking for a job as a photographer instead.

I quit my degree and landed a job as resident snapper at Butlin's Holiday Camp at Barry Island in South Wales - that's where I did my 'basic training'. I was, for all intents and purposes, a Red Coat, even though I wore a yellow, blue and green striped blazer, had hair dyed bright orange and looked like nothing more than a technicoloured six-foot clown. Despite all that, I had a fantastic time. I photographed glamorous grannies, family portraits, Miss Lovely Legs – the lot – and it proved to be the perfect grounding for my future career as a showbiz photographer.

I had a captive audience and the whole point was aimed at making money. I took the picture – two for £1.70, all of which came in an artificial plastic wallet, mind – and my commission was about 25p a job. I was working anything up to a 50-hour week and it taught me how to deal with people, get the best from them and learn what worked and what didn't.

I did one summer season lasting 20 weeks at Barry Island and after learning what an F-stop was and overcoming basic errors such as focussing correctly and using the correct setting, I started to learn the technicalities of the trade and began paying attention to detail, gradually becoming more competent as I went along and learning from my mistakes.

I knew that photography was definitely the career path I wanted to follow, but knew there was a limit to how much I could learn from being a permanent fixture at a holiday camp, so I began to expand my portfolio.

In 1979, I was staying in London and after an FA Cup final at Wembley; I decided to travel into the city with my camera to take pictures of fans celebrating in Trafalgar Square. There was a lot of energy and happiness in the pictures I took and I've always had the attitude of 'What's the worst that can happen?', so when I'd filled a couple of rolls of film, I called the Sunday Mirror's picture desk to see if they were interested. They told me to jump in a cab – they'd pay – and bring in what I had.

They took my film away, blew them up to 26 inches – the biggest I'd ever seen a photo at that point – and they chose a few images that could be laid out for the next day's back page. I thought, 'Wow – this is so easy!' Then I was suitably brought back down to earth as a TV screen in the office showed a pitch invasion taking place in the Scottish Cup Final. The picture editor kindly handed me back my pictures and said, "Sorry, Dave. Disaster always gets the edge over happiness."

They told me not to lose heart and suggested I instead keep a diary of goings on at Butlin's Barry Island. There was sex, drugs and even the apprehension of on-the-run murderers on a couple of occasions and there seemed like a decent story to be told, accompanied by whatever pictures I could take, of course.

So I returned to Butlin's and started keeping a record of various scandals and suchlike, never knowing I'd end up almost being a story myself! I became chief suspect following a robbery, one night, and I think it was that incident that convinced me it was time to pack my bags before I ended up in one of Her Majesty's holiday camps. I'd been photographing a cabaret evening – Peters and Lee if memory serves – and it was a typical chicken-in-a-basket type event that the punters thoroughly enjoyed. I was the last person out of the hall and I said goodnight to the security guard, not realising I would be the last known person to see him before he was coshed over the head prior to thieves supposedly emptying the safe.

It's amazing how quickly events seem to conspire against you and from initially dismissing the suspicion I was under, I began to think I actually might be convicted of an assault and theft I was

A selection of my favourite family photographs as I grew up in Newtown, Wales, including Mum Pat, Dad Tony, big brother Phil, my wife Janice and Mum in law.

Introduction

9

totally innocent of. Thankfully, a couple of days later the guard confessed he'd done it all himself! Apparently he'd been having an affair with a chalet maid and presumably decided to steal enough money to run off with her at some point and decided to fake a robbery. He'd emptied the safe, buried the loot at the beach and then bashed his own head on the door of the safe – you couldn't make it up! At least I was off the hook and it added another fascinating chapter to life on a holiday camp. At the end of the season I was called into the Sunday Mirror offices who told me they could use the diary and make a great story out of it. I was thinking that this was the start of my Fleet Street career and again thought, 'How easy is this?'

I scoured the paper for several weeks waiting to see my sordid exposé of Butlin's in the Sunday Mirror with no joy, then discovered the reason it hadn't been – and never would be – published. It turned out Butlin's were one of the Mirror Group's biggest advertisers and running the story would undoubtedly cost them their business. The paper made a commercial decision – 'Thou shalt not shit on thine own doorstep' – though they paid me for my troubles and wished me well. I sold it to another paper, who did exactly the same thing by paying me, but ultimately deciding it was too risky to publish.

Despite the initial disappointment, I took great heart from twice nearly having my work published and reckoned I was now a fully-fledged photographer, largely self-taught with a degree in optimism. I decided to use the money I'd made from the two unused deals to fly to the States and try my luck over there for a while. I was confident and full of verve and enthusiasm and most importantly, I wasn't afraid to ask anybody anything. In fact, I excelled at it, which any photographer will tell you is half the battle.

I called up Disneyworld in Florida and said I was a young British photographer heading over and, what with the cheap flights to America Freddie Laker was providing, I could maybe help promote Disneyworld to the people of Britain. They welcomed me with open arms and gave me some fantastic openings such as interviewing Snow White, hugging a killer whale and a host of other really touristy things that had never really been done at that time.

I submitted my pictures to an agency who sold them on for me and after having a whale of a time – literally – I returned to London in buoyant mood feeling I could do anything. I enjoyed the gimmicky aspect of the business but wanted to move towards the showbiz side a little more and with that in mind, I applied to be resident photographer at Stringfellow's nightclub, which had not long been opened and was the place to be seen in the early 1980s.

The idea was, of course, that by having an in-house snapper, the papers would never be short of a picture showing the calibre of celebrity that hung out at Stringfellow's and fortunately, I was taken on. I'd get calls at all hours of the night to rush down and take a picture of somebody – Rod Stewart one night, someone else another - and so on. I had two cameras with me; one of them for colour pictures

Introduction

Top: My early Student Union cards.

10

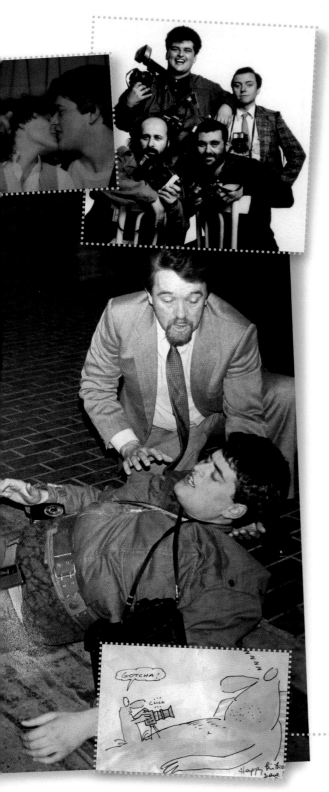

"It was an incredible time for me. I was 18, single and out clubbing every night."

destined for the hall of fame board in the foyer, so people could look at the galaxy of stars who'd been to the club, and the other with which I shot black and white pictures for the papers. Peter Stringfellow was way ahead of his time and a master of publicity and all I had to do was write the caption 'seen at London's top nightclub' on the back of every photo I sold on to the papers. It was simple and pure genius and he always looked after the journalists because he knew the value of positive publicity and good relations with the Press.

It was an incredible time for me. I was 18, single and out clubbing every night, drinking the best champagne and attending the best parties in London – what more could a young lad from the hills ask for? I had no trouble selling the pictures and as soon as I'd taken the shots, began to regularly drop my film in at The Sun's headquarters on Bouverie Street before heading off to bed at some ungodly hour.

The following day I'd invariably get a call telling me they were going to use the pictures and I'd go in and speak with the picture desk, gradually getting to know everyone fairly well. I was dealing with people who'd done a hard day's work at the paper and were basically too tired to go to any of the showbiz events or parties they'd been invited to, so they began to give them to me. I'd leave The Sun offices, often with 10 invites to various parties around the city over the next fortnight. All they really wanted was a picture they could write a brief story about and that suited me fine. I'd go along, have a drink, some decent food, take the pictures, drop

the film in and then call up the journalist in question the next day and tell them what had been going on so they could write their own version of events – it was a marriage made in heaven.

For the first five years I had to pinch myself, asking 'How can this get any better?' The money, the champagne, and the great parties – it was all free-flowing and available and I had no commitments or wife to worry about. I did what I wanted, when I wanted and it was, for me, a dream come true.

I remember parties at the Embassy Club where Freddie Mercury and Kenny Everett would be there and the whole of London's gay mafia, but even for a 23-year-old straight guy, these were the best parties you could ever go to. There was champagne available everywhere and two or three times a week I'd stay up for two or three days at a time, living the life of the people I was photographing, but still delivering the goods.

I was mainly providing pictures for John Blake's Gossip Column – one of the first of its kind that carried stories that didn't have much substance to them, rather than reporting what had been going on in the showbiz world the previous evening. It was the crazy eighties and the birth of the celebrity as we know it today and The Sun – and Peter Stringfellow, in many ways – led the way. It was quite groundbreaking stuff when you consider the public's seemingly insatiable thirst for news on celebs today and I was lucky enough to be around for the ride.

One of my most memorable moments during those colourful, hedonistic years – and one that

Main Picture: Maimed by Madonna! – the infamous event that helped to shape my career and also put me on the front pages of newspapers instead of providing the photos.

Introduction

perhaps sums up the era perfectly – ended with a picture I still love to this day, though it's not without its own sadness in many respects. I was at Stringfellow's when Oliver Reed came in with his young wife and with Olly; you just knew that at some point you would have an opportunity to get a fantastic picture of some sort. So I sat and watched as he went through one double gin and tonic after another and each time he finished, he stacked the glass on top of another and so on. It ended with him staggering back from the toilet with his shirt hanging out and fly's undone and attempting to put glass number 14 on the tower he'd built. Of course, it was just a matter of waiting for the right moment and sure enough, the glasses toppled and smashed everywhere and I caught the whole scene at just the right moment. Olly just looked over at me, completely shit-faced, half seeing me, half not with an incredulous smile. That was what my job was all about, a mixture of patience and an eye for what was likely to happen and being there to capture it when it did.

The days of photographs like that are all but gone now. Today we live in a carefully controlled world, run by PR people and bodyguards who are there to protect and make sure their employers are seen in the light they want to be seen in, which is understandable, though it's all the more boring because of that.

I've been at The Sun for 30 years now on a retainer basis, which basically means I don't work for other papers. They've been good to me and I

hope I've been good to them. They've sent me to some amazing places to cover the most incredible events and in the following pages I'll introduce you to my favourite people and the stories behind the pictures. Unforgettable experiences with incredible individuals and moments I'll never forget, for one reason or another.

The job has had a price to pay, though, because to do it properly, I had to put it before everything else in my life. You become a nocturnal creature, going to work when everyone else is coming home and rising late in the mornings. Your social life suffers and there are no hard and fast rules to play by – you pretty much make it up as you go along. I've changed family holidays to fit in photo shoots in different countries and I wasn't around as much as I'd have liked to have been when my two sons were growing up. There was insecurity and fear of missing out on a big gig, so I never turned anything down in the early years in case somebody else got the job, but having said all that, the pros far outweigh the cons.

In this game, you have to be polite and keep your word to build up trusting relationships with the people you're photographing otherwise you'll get nowhere – but that's old school thinking and there's only a few of us left with that mentality. Things have changed and there's unbelievable competition to get pictures because one image can potentially earn fortunes, but I'll always remain the same and if I'm asked not to take a picture by someone for whatever reason, I'll respect that – and they won't

Introduction

From Bizarre to Band Aid II, I have been involved with some amazing events due to my Access All Areas pass.

"It's been a rollercoaster ride, that's for sure, but one I'm very happy to be on."

Main Picture: The beautiful Kylie and I pictured at a recent event. She is one of my favourite stars to photograph.

forget it, either. Today, I'll only go to a party or whatever if I have an Access All Areas pass – if I don't get that, I don't bother because I refuse to be part of the dog-eat-dog world of snatching a picture from the pavement – it's no fun out there and I've been doing this for too long to be part of all that nonsense.

It's been a rollercoaster ride, that's for sure, but one I'm still very happy to be on. I've been knocked down by Madonna's limo at Heathrow Airport and I've walked out on stage behind Michael Jackson at his peak with 75,000 people screaming at him and tasted what it's like to be in their shoes, even for just a brief time. Moments money can't buy and taking snapshots of history – it's not been a bad life so far and I feel very privileged to have been there behind the lens, recording it all for millions of people to enjoy.

You know, I have had a recurring nightmare for 25 years which resulted in me waking up in a cold sweat, not sure whether it was real or not for a few seconds. It was me, sat behind a potter's wheel, making endless vases, and plates and god-knows-what-else, safe in the knowledge that this was my lot because it was the career I'd chosen. Today, I take a ceramics class once a week and I happily sit behind a potter's wheel and I find it very therapeutic and satisfying. It's a hobby, no more, and it reminds me how lucky I am to be doing the job I do. Thank god it's not the other way around...

Dave Hogan, London, July 2008

Introduction

★ Madonna

I used to photograph Boy George two or three times a week because at the time, he was the biggest name in pop. He changed his clothes every day and was a walking fashion statement. I was in New York with him for his birthday and he took me around these clubs with him, which were eye-openers to say the least. He had his finger on the pulse and knew exactly what was going and where it was happening and his friend Marilyn was along for the ride. George took me to the Palladium and introduced me to a girl called Madonna and he said to me, "She's going to be massive." He knew his stuff so I took a picture of her with Marilyn and she just looked like this gap-toothed 20-year-old trying to make her way – not the future of pop music for more than two decades. I took another picture of her on stage and who would have guessed that 25 years later she would still be on the front page of most newspapers every time she does something? There is nobody else who has re-invented themselves as many times as she has and continued to successfully generate that kind of press interest over such a sustained period of time. Say 'Madonna' and bang! I'll be there because whatever she does, it's going to be fascinating.

Marriage to Sean Penn

I travelled over to America for Madonna's impending marriage to firebrand actor Sean Penn, whose hatred of journalists and photography was legendary. There was no Press access whatsoever so everybody was hiring helicopters trying to find out

Madonna

"There is nobody else who has re-invented themselves as many times as she has."

where the ceremony was going to be held, but the great thing about Madonna is, if she wants to be seen, you'll see her, if she doesn't, you won't see a thing. We hired our own chopper and went to a beach at Malibu and there in the sand, written in huge letters, was the message 'F* *k off!'- nice touch from Sean Penn! A guy who I was working with, however, went to extraordinary lengths to ensure he got what he needed. Kip Rano worked for the National Enquirer and that was one magazine that made its own rules and regulations when it came to celebrities. Kip donned a white Miami Vice suit, got over the perimeter wall surrounding the venue and managed to actually get on the dance floor with Madonna and Sean. Sean went up and asked who he was and Kip said he was a friend of Madonna's so he went away. Madonna asked Sean who he was and he told her he'd said he was a friend of hers – the game was up and he was forcibly ejected after Sean wrestled him to the ground.

A little while later they were making the film 'Shanghai Surprise' together in Hong Kong and I flew out there as guests of Paula Yates and Jools Holland for the eighties music show The Tube. George Harrison's film company Handmade were making the movie and we'd been invited over to help promote the film. I went over with The Sun reporter, Martin Dunn now Editor-in-Chief of the New York Daily News, and as we were flying in, we were told the unit publicity person had been sacked and nobody knew if our meeting had been scrapped or not. We sat around for three or four days with no

Madonna

15

"There have been constant rumours that Madonna's marriage to Guy Ritchie is in trouble."

worked, I might be talking about Christina and Britney instead, but it wasn't to be.

There was another time when I was waiting backstage at 'Top of the Pops' as she promoted her album 'Ray of Light' and I waited until she came off stage to see if I could get anything interesting. As she approached, she said, "Do you mind if I go and get changed?" She was wearing a black dress and looked fantastic, but she added, "I know how you tabloids like your colour and I've got just the coat." With that, she went away for a few moments and then came back in this fantastically coloured coat, carrying her daughter, Lourdes. I knew this was a very valuable shot, but she then asked me not to take any shots of Lourdes, and of course, I didn't. She put Lourdes down, but as she did, their hair grips entangled and she got down on her knees to free the knot. I asked if I could help but she said they'd be fine. There was a few moments when it was just mother and daughter sorting out a minor problem and I felt very privileged to have witnessed it.

Madonna & Guy

We knew there'd be no access at the wedding itself, but we were allowed one picture of Rocco's Christening the day before when Madonna and Guy, plus all the guests posed for a picture on the steps of the church. We knew that'd be it and we wouldn't see them again and it shows the level of loyalty and commitment from their friends, family and staff that there has never been a single picture published of that wedding. They didn't need the added exposure

and I think that shows the respect and esteem they are both held in.

In the year's in-between that day, there have been constant rumours that Madonna's marriage to Guy Ritchie is in trouble, but that's never something I've ever seen evidence of. They are two strong characters and Guy won't pander to anyone, so there are bound to be moments of friction, so when I got to go and prove they were still very much in love, I wasn't about to turn it down. There was a story appearing the next day in a rival paper claiming the marriage was on the rocks and Madonna's camp were keen to make the story look nonsense. I was told where they'd be and the time they'd be there, but I wasn't happy waiting outside on the pavement. I waited in my car until I got a call that they'd be out in few moments, but Guy wasn't playing the game and rushed to a waiting car leaving

Madonna

Madonna alone in the doorway of the restaurant. She shrugged and I said, "Goodnight, then." Not long after, at The Brits, I was escorted to their table to take a picture of them together, but they were sat apart. I said, "You're not together – you're sitting at one end and you're at the other." There was an awkward moment until Madonna finally said, "Well I suppose I'd better get up then, hadn't I?" She walked over and sat next to Guy and because they weren't touchy-feely, I still didn't photograph them. Finally, they got closer and I took the picture, but it wasn't as easy as it should have been. Time will tell and I hope they'll prove the doubters wrong – we'll have to wait and see.

Madonna

ACCESS ALL AREAS

Simon Cowell

There are lots and lots of people who tell you 'this is the next big thing', but most of them never are so you tend to take the majority of tips for great things with a pinch of salt. The one person you do listen to in this industry is Simon Cowell, because if he says someone is going to be big, they already are and he just makes them bigger. He works very well with the media and knows what they want and how to deliver the goods and you need people like him in this business.

I was over at his house in Los Angeles one time, with Rav Singh (Simon's best mate) and Victoria Newton while he was on the panel for 'American Idol' in the States and he asked us to listen to a CD. He played what sounded a bit like The Three Tenors – it turned out to be Il Divo, long before they'd come to the attention of the public. He said, "These will be massive." And of course, now they are.

Cowell can spot talent at a very early and raw stage – that's what he does and that's what he's exceptional at. Normally, on the night that the 'Pop Idol', 'Britain's Got Talent' or 'X-Factor' winners are announced, I will go down to the TV studio and shoot the first set of pictures. I've photographed Girls Aloud, G4, Leon Jackson, Leona Lewis – the list goes on. I think the only time things went horribly wrong was with the first 'X-Factor' winner Steve Brookstein back in 2005, but overall, Cowell's judgement is second-to-none and he's been involved with Five, Westlife and dozens of others.

It must be difficult having people come up and tell you that they are going to be the next big thing

Simon Cowell

"Cowell can spot talent at a very early and raw stage."

all the time and I've had countless unknown artists asking me to photograph them because they were about to be discovered and I probably get 20 or 30 calls a month from various bands or their managers. Most of them, sadly, disappear and you never see them again, but occasionally, they are right. I was at a Duran Duran party when this guy came up and said, "We're going to be big." I thought, 'here we go'. I said, "Really?" He said, "Yeah, we're going to be really big. Our single will be out next month and after that, we'll be huge." I decided to pass on the opportunity and a month later, 'Take On Me' went to No. 1 in the UK and USA and, just as Morten Harket had predicted, A-ha became massive. Oh well... can't win them all. From that day on, however, Morten remembered me and the next time we met, he said, "As punishment for ignoring me, you can only shoot me in black and white today."

Returning to Simon Cowell, I recall when I sold the company I'd built up to Getty Images, he was really interested in the deal and asked me a load of questions and then said, "You've done really well, Dave." That meant a hell of a lot to me because he's got one of the sharpest business brains around and if he thought I'd done well, that was good enough for me.

He shows no sign of fading into the background, either, and has groomed Leona Lewis from being a quiet mouse-like little girl who everybody thought was ordinary and boring, into an Americanised, polished diamond who is now selling millions of records around the world. Simon's got a very long shelf life ahead of him because he has the Midas Touch, he makes things happen and good luck to him.

Simon Cowell

Louis Walsh
& Reality TV Stars

You can't mistake Hogie – he stands out a mile, turns up everywhere and most importantly, gets great pictures. Hogie is always laughing and is great fun and you can see that he enjoys his job immensely – and I think that shows in his work. He knows, to a certain extent, that he holds a privileged position and you don't remain The Sun's showbiz photographer for 25 years if you don't know your stuff.

I've managed bands like Boyzone, Westlife and Girls Aloud and wherever they have appeared over the years, you can bet Hogie would be there amid hundreds of screaming girls with a big grin on his face – no wonder!

He's loads of fun and both myself and Simon Cowell have worked with him many, many times over the years and we've always had a good laugh together. He's cheerful, professional and comes in and gets his stuff done with a minimum of fuss – most importantly, the artists all respect him and like him taking their picture and I'm not sure there are many photographer's around who you could say that of.

He has the eye and always captures the magic moment – he delivers the goods time after time and he has an uncanny knack of making things look better than they actually were at the time and for me, that's a rare talent.

Hogie always delivers the goods and is the man I want photographing the bands I manage – I can't give him higher praise than that. He's a nice guy, a character and everybody loves him and by the end of this book, you'll know exactly why he's stayed at the top of the tree for so long – here's to another 25 years!

Louis Walsh, Dublin, July 2008

Louis Walsh

ACCESS **ALL** AREAS

Louis Walsh

23

Take That

The first picture I ever took of Take That is still one of their most well-known. Peter Willis was at the time working on the Bizarre column at The Sun and he wanted to know how we were going to get this new boy band that nobody had heard of in the paper. St Valentine's Day was coming up so he suggested we get them stripped off wearing nothing but their boxer shorts and in turn, we could promote the boxers as Valentine gifts for boyfriends. We hired a studio and Take That came along, stripped down to their boxers and we had a great afternoon, just messing around and getting some terrific shots. There wasn't one tattoo among them and they were clearly clean-cut lads not long out of school.

The pictures were great, but we couldn't get them in the paper – it was very disappointing, but that's life and you move on. Three months later, however, and it was a different story. Take That went to Number One in The Singles Charts and suddenly everyone wanted their picture so I went to America with them to cover their first trip across the Atlantic. They went from Los Angeles to New York, where the temperature was minus one and all they had on were these flimsy denim jackets and T-shirts – they were freezing. We hired a limo and did the quickest photo shoot possible with the lads in front of all the major landmarks before they jumped back in the limo where the heating was on full. We finished for the day and I went off to process the films. As I walked back across Time Square, I saw somebody attack a guy across the face with a knife – literally

Take That

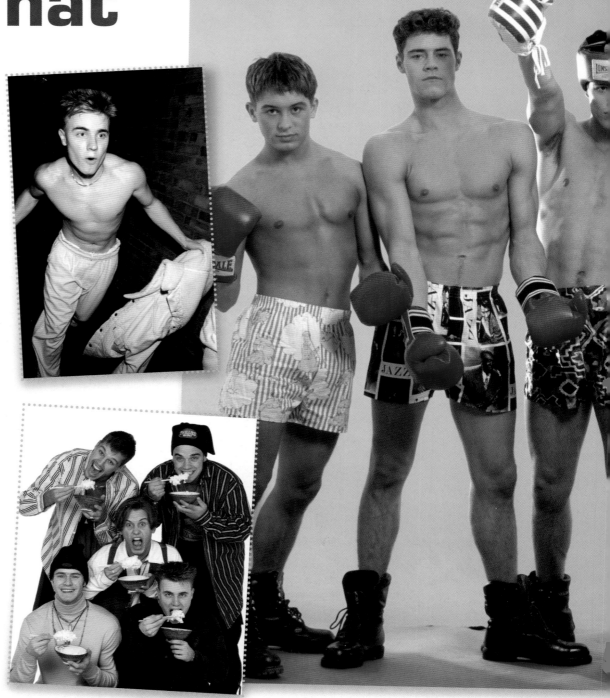

"There wasn't a tattoo among them and they were clearly clean-cut lads."

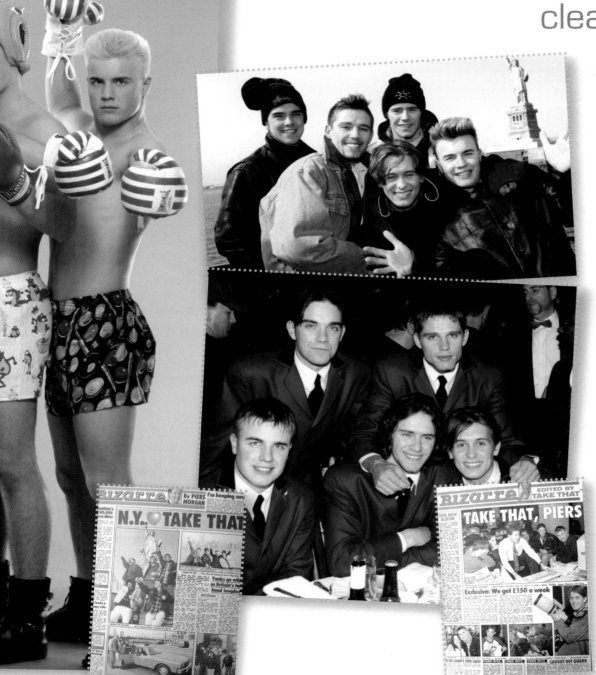

right in front of me. It was a terrible thing to witness, but I had my camera and instinctively took two or three frames. The guy was treated and then taken away in an ambulance and I had the pictures developed and took them back to show the lads. I told them what had happened and they were fascinated by both the story and the pictures. They hadn't really done anything at that point of much interest, so they adopted my story as their own – they'd witnessed the attack personally and they relayed it during interviews as their 'New York Story'.

From there we went to Japan and initially, they were fairly unknown on their arrival, but word soon spread pretty quickly and nobody envisaged the pandemonium that followed. I ended up being photographer, security and TV footage cameraman (for Andy Peters' 'O-Zone' kid's programme because his show didn't have the budget to send their own man!) It all got a bit out of hand and eventually the record company hired a load of security guys to come in and help them. It was fantastic to be there at the beginning of the Take That hysteria and I watched it develop almost before my own eyes. It was a great time and they were a good set of lads who deserved their success.

I remember doing a set of pictures with Howard Donald after the split and he came down to London, we did the pictures and afterwards he said, "You know for a year after the band broke up, I didn't get out of bed until noon. I had no reason to get up and would lie in bed watching 'Richard and Judy'. I'd done all those things and all of a sudden you're not

Take That

"When the band reformed, the hysteria was just as wild."

fashionable and nobody wants to take your call. How cruel is this world?"

I did some nice pictures of Gary Barlow when he got married and then he suddenly spilled the beans about all the women and drugs he'd had over the years, but it just didn't sound right coming from him. Gary was always the talented musician who'd done the working men's clubs and served his apprenticeship, but he was always dubbed 'the fat one from Take That'. When the band reformed, the hysteria was just as wild despite the guys and their fans being 10 years older – it was electrifying and the gigs they played were incredible.

They did a show where their opening number consisted of three minutes of almost X-rated lap dancing with Mark and Gary gyrating and you could see they were having fun. I did a set of pictures with them near to Christmas 2007 and as I was sat chatting with Gary he said, "You know what, we're going to enjoy it this time. The first time was just a whirlwind of hotels, girls and parties but we savour every moment now." And they are. The ironic thing was that there was a part of the show where they were singing while running on a treadmill at full speed. I was watching them and could see that of all the lads, only Gary wasn't sweating. The others all looked like they'd had 20 fags and were struggling, but it was the so-called 'fat one' who was leading the way. Afterwards, Gary told me he had a personal running trainer and he's now a lean, mean, fighting machine and good luck to him. Some things really do come full circle, don't they?

Take That

26

Robbie Williams

Very few boy bands ever grow up to be man bands – it just doesn't happen. I've seen them come and I've seen them go and my advice to any of the boy bands I've worked with is to put something aside from that first royalty cheque. When Take That split up as a foursome with a final appearance at The Brits, it must have been a tremendous anti-climax for them all, having tasted the high life for so long and having had such adulation poured on them by their legion of fans for so long.

Of course, Robbie Williams then went off on his own to Barbados to take stock of his life and then Bizarre editor Andy Coulson agreed with Robbie's PR people to allow me to travel over and cover the trip. The deal was that the paper paid for the whole gig and in return, we got a series of exclusive postcards in return.

Robbie flew out on Concorde and I went out in economy – in case I needed a reality check – and I caught up with him at his hotel in Barbados. Robbie had never had to think for himself before and had nobody telling him what his daily schedule should be and he was essentially on his own, with no record company, no career plan – nothing – other than plenty of time on his hands.

He was always fooling around, playing football, and pinching my mini-moke or whatever while I took the pictures. I remember sitting in the bar with him as he scribbled lyrics down and he'd turn and say "What do you think of this Dave?" or "Is this any good?" Bernie Taupin I ain't and I'd never been in a situation where someone confided in me so much.

Robbie Williams

"His life had moved at lightning pace and relaxation was not on the agenda."

He was excited about the future one moment, bewildered the next and it was hard to keep up with him at times.

Always interesting to photograph, I got some great pictures – one of him lounging in a white suit, another with a ball and chain around his leg and a number of other concepts we devised between us. Whatever he did, he did it at 100mph and eventually I said, "have you ever just sat down and read a book?" He told me he hadn't and I wasn't surprised. His life had moved at lightning pace and relaxation was not on the agenda.

Meanwhile, my old mate Piers Morgan left The Sun and went to edit The Mirror and being a family friend, he called my house and spoke to my son Josh. "Where's daddy?" he asked – and, of course, he told Uncle Piers I was in Barbados with Robbie Williams. The Mirror then sent a team of journalists over to try and find me, before working out I was in the same hotel as Robbie.

Patsy Kensit flew out after a few days – she was a friend of Robbie's then girlfriend, Jacqui Hamilton-Smith, who was celebrating her birthday. For the party, we hired a yacht for the day, complete with its own crew and sailed around the island. The champagne flowed freely and the day ended up with a mass chocolate cake fight with everyone smearing cake in each other's faces – totally childish, but terrific fun and all recorded for prosperity by yours truly.

Robbie Williams

ACCESS
ALL
AREAS

We ended up in Patsy's hotel room and at that point, the lobster, the champagne and the seasickness all sloshed together, the colour completely drained from my face and I made my excuses, headed for the toilet and coated everywhere with projectile vomit! When it was over, I tried desperately to clean it all up, mopping here, soaking there and spraying expensive perfume everywhere trying to cover my tracks.

The following morning Patsy called me up and asked if I was okay. I said I was fine. "Really, Dave? Only I found sick sprayed underneath the toilet seat..." Guilty as charged! Another time, I was in Patsy's hotel room when a fax started to come through from Liam Gallagher, who was seeing her at the time. We scrawled a few messages and sent it back to Liam – what he made of me being in his girlfriend's hotel room at 3am in the morning, god only knows, but it was only a bit of harmless fun.

There was never a dull moment with Robbie who was always the joker, always the life and soul of the party, but unfortunately, it didn't last. We fell out a few years later and things have never really been the same since. I received a call saying that Robbie was going to attend to watch his mate, Jonathan Wilkes, who was appearing in The Rocky Horror Show. It was the opening night and I was sent along to get a few pics of Robbie, which would in turn promote the show. By

Robbie Williams

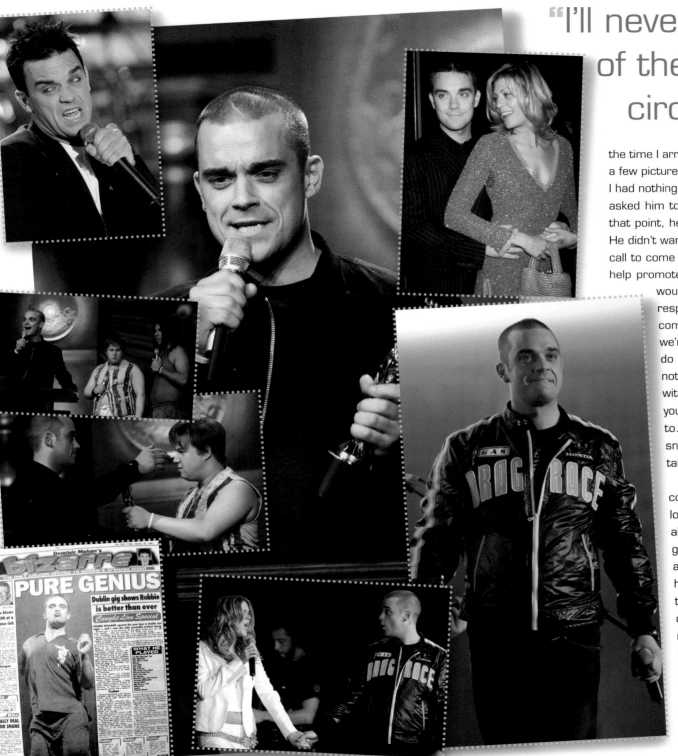

"I'll never be part of the inner circle again."

the time I arrived, he'd already gone in and had had a few pictures taken by other photographers, while I had nothing, During the break, I found Robbie and asked him to pose for a couple of frames, but by that point, he had what I call his 'serious face' on. He didn't want to do it so I said, "Robbie, I've had a call to come down here from Jonathan's people to help promote this. They told us you'd be here and would pose for a shot with him. With respect, we wouldn't have bothered coming otherwise – he's your mate and we're only here because you are – will you do a few pictures?" He said he'd rather not and I said, "Well I'd rather be at home with my family, but I've come out because your mate's management has asked me to." He stood there in his vest, almost snarling and grudgingly allowed me to take a picture.

His people called me later to complain and Robbie personally left a long rant on my home answer phone about my insistence that he played the game on that evening, but I wasn't about to apologise. I've photographed him since, but I know I'll never be part of the inner circle again – you go in and out of favour with Robbie and you never really know where you stand with him, but he's one of the biggest stars in the world and hopefully I will get to work closely with him again.

Robbie Williams

31

Boybands

Boybands

Main Picture: The new and improved Boyzone. **From left to right clockwise:** Boyzone in what would be their last concert until the reunion, Bros, New Kids on the Block (old and new), NSYNC, Backstreet Boys, Westlife, Busted, McFly, East 17 and Blue.

"Dave is a great guy. We worked with him right from the beginning with Boyzone, then with all my solo stuff and more recently again when Boyzone reformed, Dave was the first guy to shoot us. As well as being a great photographer he's a top bloke to be around. He was really nice to us before we were famous which doesn't happen that often, normally people get nice when the success comes along.." **Ronan Keating**

ACCESS **ALL** AREAS

Boybands

Michael Jackson

I first photographed Michael Jackson when he was in Kansas City with the Jackson 5. I flew out and it was a magical moment because you could never watch Michael perform without him blowing your socks off. He came on, looked great, did his stuff and everything seemed to be going well for him and his brothers.

In 1983, he came to London and I had a one-to-one chat with him for the first time. He was with his friends, Paul and Linda McCartney, at the BPI Awards (now 'The Brits') and he walked into the room and I took a picture of all three of them together. Then the main focus shifted to the McCartneys, but I decided to stick with Michael who was on his own, standing with a bodyguard in the corner.

I went over and tried to be friendly, welcoming him to London and making small-talk, but he was all-but ignoring me. I asked if I could take one or two pictures and he said, "Yeah, sure." The picture I took shows him with the nose he was born with, he is black, has had no plastic surgery and he looks amazing. About 10 minutes later he walked over to me and asked if I'd take some pictures of him with his friends, which of course I was more than happy to do. He posed with Pete Townshend, Eric Clapton and about a half-a-dozen others and the next day I dropped in a big pile of pictures at his hotel and then didn't see him for a while.

When 'Thriller' came out, I flew out to New York and took various shots of Michael and his friends. I took one with Brooke Shields, who later revealed that her mother was invoicing Michael's people

Michael Jackson

"I'd get asked to come along and take pictures as he bought a Winnie the Pooh lunchbox."

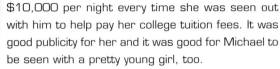

$10,000 per night every time she was seen out with him to help pay her college tuition fees. It was good publicity for her and it was good for Michael to be seen with a pretty young girl, too.

There was one time I went to photograph him at an event at the Natural History Museum in New York where everyone was given a white glove and a list of things we could or couldn't do when taking his pictures – the first indications that working with Michael would never be less than bizarre – but every time he was on stage, he was electric and just blew the crowd away. It was clear he was special and had a presence about him and thanks to a guy called Jonathan Morrish who worked at CBS records, I'd get called up from time to time and began to get special access to Michael. If he went shopping at Hamley's in London, I'd get asked to come along and take pictures as he bought a Winnie the Pooh lunchbox, DVDs, toys or whatever and there would invariably be dozens of Japanese tourists following him around in suitable awe. I'd take shots of him with Lisa Marie Presley if they were over here, though notably, there'd never be a chance to get some shots of him with his wife, Debbie.

Things went a little pear-shaped after The Mirror published a front page picture of Michael with his face seemingly flaking off, but that was never anything I set out to get. I was intrigued by the mystery and magic of Michael Jackson the performer, even though you could see something had clearly gone on with his facial features.

I used to say Michael Jackson bought my

Porsche because my special access meant any pictures I took were in great demand, particularly in America, and the money rolled in. For a time, everything he touched turned to gold, but of course, the storm clouds lay on the horizon.

I was at the World Music Awards when Jordy Chandler was sat on Michael's knee with Prince Albert and a host of supermodels around him. Michael was bouncing Jordy, then aged 13, up and down on his knee and it just didn't look right and I've always wondered why somebody didn't tell him as much. All the people earning big money from being around him, advising him or whatever and nobody thinks to say, 'You know what, Michael? You're inviting trouble and that kind of behaviour is unacceptable.'

In 1997, I flew to Germany, met his manager and eventually met Michael. I went into a room, shook his hand and, for want of a better description, he sniffed me – though I think it was more due to the breathing problems he was reportedly having. Either way, that's how it felt. He left the room shortly after and then 10 minutes later somebody came in and said I was OK to shoot the show. I flew back to London in preparation for the concert a few days later and when I returned to Germany, I was taken into Michael's quick-change dressing room, which is basically a tent at the side of the stage with a big flight case containing make-up and various tools of the trade with huge mirrors around it.

A silver-haired guy came in and was showing me all the various accessories Michael used on stage

Michael Jackson

and I got to try on the Thriller hat, the diamond glove and felt very privileged, though they were just props when I tried them on – they didn't attain the magic until Michael used them on stage. I was pinching myself that I'd been admitted into the inner sanctum of the biggest artist in the world. Then Michael pops in, changes costume, sprays deodorant under his arms and starts putting some make-up on – it was totally surreal. I shot 56 rolls of film that day and there is image after image of Michael, all fantastic stuff that The Sun whittled down to a three-page spread.

The most incredible thing of all was when he went out on stage. I was stood right behind him as he came out of a spaceship, then the smoke poured around him and the stage lights came up – and I'm stood there with him as 75,000 fans go crazy. The noise was hitting him and bouncing on to me and in an instant, you experience that unique, incredible high that these guys get every time they perform and trust me, there's no drug around that could ever come close to that rush.

In later years I won an award for a picture I took of Michael, there was another time when he came out of Madame Tussauds and stood on top of his car because he wanted to wave to his fans. Nobody knew he was going to do that and I was lucky enough to be in the right place at the right time.

Today, after all that's happened, I'm not sure Michael will ever recover – one of the latest pictures I have of him shows him looking as almost a grotesque caricature of what he once was and it is

Michael Jackson

"Today he is a social pariah, homeless with his career in shreds."

probably the definitive 'Just Say No To Plastic Surgery' image you're ever likely to see. It later transpired some of the surgeons had treated Michael badly and took the money, taking advantage of his nature and wealth while doing what were in effect sub-standard jobs.

Today, he is a social pariah, homeless with his career in shreds. The vultures have moved on and he has astronomical debts, but I, for one, hope he comes back. As for the allegations against him, I can only think from my own view as a parent, and that is that if you really thought there was the slightest possibility of abuse taking place, you don't let your kid go to his house. Surely you'd rather cut your own hand off rather than accept money for something that might or might not have taken place. It would be prosecution or nothing because no amount of money could ever put something as terrible as that right and there are a lot of questions that need to be asked of a lot of parents' motives where it concerns friendships with Michael Jackson.

Michael Jackson

The Spice Girls

Capital Radio held an annual road show and that was where I met five young ladies who together formed The Spice Girls. For some reason, I expected them to be all gobby individuals, all desperate to grab the limelight but was pleasantly surprised. The term 'Girl Power' had just started being bandied around and their timing was perfect because most newspaper picture desks, at least at that time, were dominated by males and The Spice Girls seemed to appeal to various picture editors, though it seemed they all liked a different one. That made it difficult to know who to focus on when taking pictures of them – do you do a group shot then concentrate on Geri because she was wearing something outrageous? Posh Spice, Baby Spice, Mel B? One thing was for sure, because Mel C always wore a tracksuit, she was the last picture I'd take because she'd be dressed the least visually interesting of the five.

There was an incident very early on in their career that convinced me these girls would go far. I was out partying with Andy Coulson, editor of the Bizarre column at the time and it was about 4am in the morning and we were still singing songs from various musicals. The next day, we were both worse for wear and Andy calls and reminds me we have to go and meet The Spice Girls – 'the next big thing' – but Andy felt rotten and decided to postpone the interview and photo shoot. Unfortunately, he'd met his match because these girls weren't about to take 'no' for an answer and they decided to come and visit Andy on his sickbed! They turned up at his house and

The Spice Girls

**"They were different
and running
on raw energy."**

ACCESS
ALL
AREAS

were bouncing around on his bed and he then called me up telling me to get around quickly and get some shots – you didn't cancel The Spice Girls, apparently!

They were different and running on raw energy because they didn't have stylists or anything like that – they were just full of belief in themselves, utterly determined to get to the top and most of all, they were great fun to be around. They filled a gap in the market and for a long time, they dominated it and could do no wrong and the term Girl Power belonged to them.

There was one set of pictures I took of them where they are all naked on Christine Keeler chairs that looked fantastic and at The Brits, Geri wore that Union Jack dress and you thought, 'Yeah, they've got it.' It wasn't about lavish expense, just clever marketing and original ideas.

They were up for anything and we had a lot of fun when they shot a video for their World Cup song. Another time, they went to Cannes to promote 'Spice World -The Movie' and they were all dressed in headscarves with roses to recreate the fifties glamour look and they stole the show. They knew how to play the game because they knew what it was all about. I wondered how things would pan out for the girls, especially after one shoot where I took pictures of one of their concerts and Geri Halliwell was on rollerblades when she suddenly looked at me right in the eyes and burst into tears. I turned to the publicity guy and asked if I'd done something wrong and he said he didn't know. What I didn't know at the time was that Geri had decided

The Spice Girls

"In 2007 they returned, still looking fantastic, but different."

to leave the band and did so after that show. I went out to Sweden for their first performance as a foursome and they did well and then I went over to America with them, too. I was in Miami when David Beckham became a hate figure in England after being red carded against Argentina during the 1998 World Cup. The remaining girls called it a day not long after that, so I'd been there at the beginning and at the end.

I still did various stuff with the girls as individuals. Mel B had her baby, but we'd agreed not to photograph the baby, despite the offer of huge money from magazines desperate to get something. While I was there, Mel asked if I could do the baby's passport picture, which I did. That picture, at that moment, was worth about £100,000, but of course I was never going to do anything other than process it and give it back to Mel, who'd agreed that money earned from syndicated pictures of her baby would go to St James' University Hospital in Leeds.

I was in Barbados and making my way back to the hotel after a scuba diving trip when I glanced at a tattoo on a women's leg. I recognised it and looked up to see it belonged to Mel C who was relaxing on a sun-lounger. She asked what I was doing there and I asked the same thing. I said, "I bet you've been papped." She nodded and said, "Look over there." There were four photographers crouching behind a bush and I had to smile. I was on holiday; just like she was so I told her I'd see her again and went on my way.

The Spice Girls

I did various projects with Geri after the split and on one occasion Chris Evans came in with her, though I had no idea why at the time. He was saying "She's alright, isn't she?" to me and I was like, "Yeah, she's gorgeous!" – never knowing they were an item at the time. There was another photo shoot when she looked fantastic and brought her dog with her. She asked for a picture with the dog and bent down to lift its ears up – her boobs almost fell out and I had to avert my attention. It would have been an amazing shot, but you can never abuse your position so I waited and left well alone. She always did visually stunning things and is a delight for any photographer because she is never less than interesting.

In 2007 they returned, still looking fantastic, but different. Some of them were mothers; some had enjoyed some solo successes but just like Take That, they'd recaptured the moment and had come back bigger and better than life thanks to Alan Edwards who had orchestrated their great PR comeback. I was at their concert in Vancouver and to their credit, they weren't there to promote a new album – they just did their greatest hits and gave their fans what they wanted so from the moment they struck the first chord, they couldn't fail. I enjoyed it as much as the crowd.

The Spice Girls

41

Posh & Becks

She picked me out of a sticker boo
...I chose her from a music vide

Going back to the eighties, Duran Duran always seemed to have thumbed through the latest supermodel catalogue and got their people to contact the models' to see if they wanted to get together. It was a sort of elite dating game of the top pop stars and the top models and I think that's probably how Victoria and David Beckham became an item. She'd seen him playing football, he'd seen her on Top of the Pops, they liked each other so they get together and it all becomes this sort of fairytale dream.

I was very fortunate to be asked to go up to the hotel where they were going to get engaged – but the pressure was on. They didn't want a Hello!-type shoot so we did pictures in and around the hotel and you could see they were like two teenagers in love. They were all over each other, totally besotted with one another and it was all very sweet.

One of the pictures that really worked well was of their hands together, showing off their diamond engagement rings. It ran the following day and the big story became finding out where they'd got these fantastic rings from. All the top jewellers in this country denied they'd made them and it transpired they'd bought the gems in America – and forgotten to declare them on their return to Manchester! I think it cost them about £15,000 in duty and in hindsight, I would imagine they'd rather have not had that particular shot taken – but that's the price of fame.

The pictures ran in OK magazine and they bought exclusive rights to them which was a

Posh & Becks

"He was obviously well trained in projecting a certain look and had a half smile."

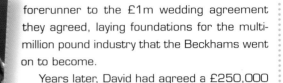

forerunner to the £1m wedding agreement they agreed, laying foundations for the multi-million pound industry that the Beckhams went on to become.

Years later, David had agreed a £250,000 deal to write a column in the News of the World eight times a year, but it hadn't been specified in the contract what he would or wouldn't do picture-wise. I was told to get him to wear this, do that and so on so I travelled up to Manchester with loads of gear in different sizes, sorted a studio out and the picture desk had created a list of ideas for images. I showed his people the list and they said no to practically all of it so I asked what he would actually do. They told me he would wear his own clothes plus an England top and a few other pics. He was obviously well trained in projecting a certain look and had a half smile so I said, "I'll get you to smile properly before we finish." He said, "No you won't," but I insisted I would. At the end, I told him he had something on the corner of his mouth and tapped his cheek and he broke out in a wide smile and I quickly took the pictures. He told me he didn't want to use the image and I asked why not? "Because Victoria says I look like Pug from The Bash Street Kids when I smile," he replied. Of course, he doesn't look like Pug – he has a lot of charisma about him. He didn't wear any of the clothes I'd brought, but he took them away with him at the end! The picture editor told me he'd deduct it from his fee, but I don't know if he ever did.

Posh & Becks

Britney Spears

I think the first time I photographed Britney Spears was over in Philadelphia for one of her opening tour shows. She was trying to grow up and create a much edgier, adult image which was understandable – I have some pictures of her looking like a Barbie Doll playing seven-year-old music that was fit for kids' birthday parties and not much else.

Then she had a photo call in Paris at The Eiffel Tower, still looking like the girl next door with very little make-up on looking anything but a sex symbol. But, of course, all that was about to change in one of the most public falls from grace in recent times.

A few years later at the MTV awards, she came out on stage wearing a suit and I was wondering what she could possibly do that would create any interest when she suddenly starts to perform a striptease! It was like, "I'm a grown-up, now. I've got boobs and I'm gonna shake them." From that moment on, she became front page news. Having successfully shed the whiter-than-white innocent schoolgirl image to become the young sex goddess in waiting, she embarked on a rollercoaster ride that is still out of control. She started seeing Justin Timberlake, too, who was with N-Sync at the time and looking a bit nerdy, so in that sense, they were a well-suited Mr & Mrs Clean-cut Teenage America – it was the Disney Club one step up, but they eventually split and went in different directions.

From there on, Britney went into decline and a lot of the people who had carefully guided her from kids TV to pop princess and had done a terrific job

Britney Spears

ACCESS **ALL** AREAS

in the process, were cast aside and she ended up marrying on a whim and left needing to perform one outrageous stunt after another to maintain interest from the press and public alike. Some of it worked, like snogging Madonna and Christina Aguilera and coming on with a boa constrictor at the MTV awards in New York, but when you keep pushing back the boundaries in desperation, it's a slippery road down straight on to the button marked self-destruct.

I spoke to a guy in America and he told me Britney has 20 cars following her every move and I feel it can only end in tragedy, though I hope for her sake it doesn't. The obsession from the media in America is frightening and the boundaries our industry is supposed to adhere to have been crossed a long time ago when it comes to Britney coverage. It's time to step back, let her get herself together and allow her the opportunity to come back and entertain people again for all the right reasons – or the next big story could also be her last.

Britney Spears

Christina Aguilera

Christina Aguilera

One of the most stunning and photogenic women in the world today, always a show-stopper!

Christina Aguilera

Paul McCartney

There can't be too many people in the world who haven't been influenced in some way by the music of The Beatles. Paul McCartney, with Bono, are probably my ultimate heroes, so when I finally got the opportunity to photograph Macca, it was quite a thrill.

During the early eighties, I went along to a Linda McCartney photographic exhibition at Hamilton's in London. I did some pictures of Paul and Linda together and then picked a portrait lens up and asked Paul if I could do a picture of him. He said I could and then proceeded to contort his face at the lens to give me one of the most spontaneous, memorable images I've ever taken.

For years after, Paul would hold a Buddy Holly Day because he'd bought the rights to his back catalogue. I remember getting a call inviting me to the event and Paul and Linda would come along dressed as Buddy Holly with guests all wearing Teddy Boy togs and looking fantastic.

Paul and Linda were one of the great love stories of modern times and they were virtually never apart, so I took a number of pictures of them both over the years. I travelled to various destinations, but one of the best was when Paul was allowed back into Japan, having previously been banned following a drugs conviction. Jeff Baker, Macca's legendary PR guy, invited me along to get pictures of the Japanese gigs and it was a privilege to be involved. Macca's a very down-to-earth guy with not even the merest hint of a superstar tantrum in him and it was incredibly sad when he

Paul McCartney

> "Macca's a very down-to-earth guy with not even the merest hint of superstar tantrum in him."

lost his soul-mate to cancer in 1998.

About a year after Linda died, I went along to Paul's office in Soho and I took a portrait of him standing up against a huge picture of Linda and he was talking passionately about the cookery book she'd written, but he rarely took his hand out of his pocket. He obviously was holding something and when his hand came out, I asked him what it was. He opened his palm to reveal Linda's wedding ring and I realised at that moment just how much he must have been missing his wife and in all honesty, I would have liked to have just gone up to him and given him a big hug. Jeff Baker told me he kept the ring with him at all times and I imagine he misses her as much today as he did then, perhaps more so in view of recent events.

There was another time when I was invited to a Rock and Roll Hall of Fame event in New York with Bizarre editor Dominic Mohan where they were honouring Macca. Stella McCartney went on stage wearing an 'About F*****g Time Too' T-shirt. I got some good shots and then we were invited backstage to interview Paul and get some more pictures. One of Macca's entourage then came up and asked if I'd like a drink, which then resulted in me going on a bender. The following day I had to do a St Patrick's Day shoot with Irish girl band B*witched where they wore green hats, green jackets while drinking green pints of Guinness – the trouble was, I was greener than all of them put together. Still suffering the effects of my mega session, I took all the pictures out of focus so they

Paul McCartney

could only be used as the size of a postage stamp. When the effects wore off, I decided then and there that I would never work 'under the influence' again.

I was also at a 9/11 fundraising event for the New York Fire Department in Madison Square Garden and in America, Paul McCartney is God – full-stop. It was an emotionally-charged day and I learned that security forces were half-expecting a terrorist attack that day and there was a lot of paranoia around and while each artist did their set, each family member who'd lost a loved one in the atrocity held up their picture. It was a very emotional day. Paul was, by that time, with Heather Mills and everything seemed to be going along well.

I took a couple of frames of them together at the VE Day concert in Trafalgar Square where Heather is all dolled up but Paul has this old jacket on that your granddad might wear carrying two VE Day flags! That was, for me at least, the first time I'd really been aware of the sizeable age gap. The next time I saw them together, was when they were stood at the side of a stage watching a U2 concert and you could sense there was something wrong and there was a tension of some kind. Paul was happy to do pics with Bono, but when he was asked to pose for a picture with his wife, she was very prickly. Of course, now they've divorced and I don't think anybody is particularly saddened by the split.

Paul McCartney

"Paul McCartney is God – full-stop."

On a happier note, Macca was also honoured at the 2008 Brits with a Lifetime Achievement award – about time too!

Paul McCartney

The Krays

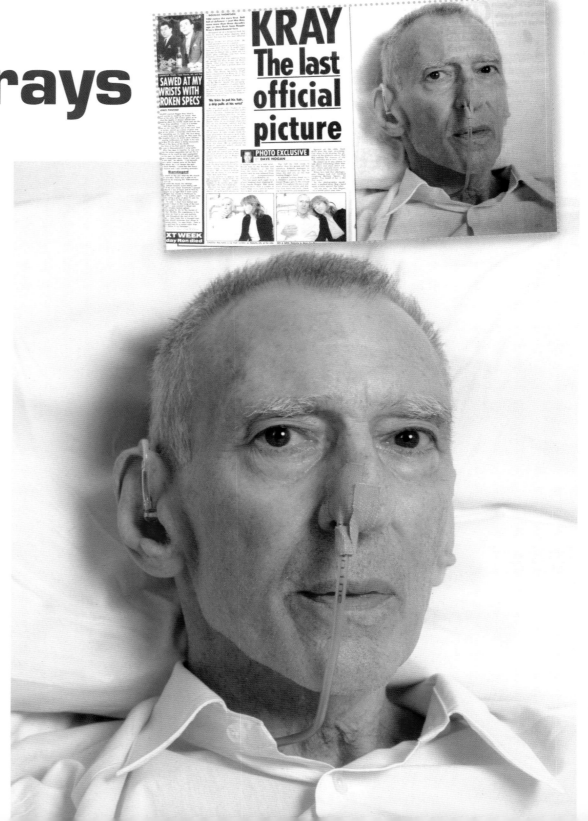

It was after I'd been awarded Entertainment Photographer of the Year that I first had contact from The Krays. I was invited to come and meet Reggie Kray who was then still a strong influence in the East End of London. When Ronnie died, I was asked to go along and take some pictures of Reggie and his family and friends so I went along to meet him at the chapel of rest. They wanted me to do a picture of the three brothers stood over the body and my preparation the night before was for my ex-wife Caroline to lie on the floor with white make-up on as I worked out how we could get three people around the coffin in order to make a shape that would work.

So I arrived all prepared with an idea for the picture, but the copper who was handcuffed to Reggie wouldn't allow him to open the coffin and in all honesty, I was quite relieved! The chain was visible in all the pictures I took and one of them was of the four main London gangs, all united over Ronnie's coffin as well as various other shots.

The whole funeral was about gangland respect and I was invited to travel in one of the family cars as the funeral cortege made its way to the cenotaph. The horse and cart carrying Ronnie passed the Krays' mother's house and my driver was positioned towards the back of a long line of cars. I called him to tell him I was OK and didn't need him to take me so at one point, he peeled off to drive onto the cenotaph, but little did I know until the news that evening of the ensuing chaos that call had caused.

The Krays

"I was graveside at the burial and could feel eyes menacingly looking at me wondering why a photographer was there."

As aerial shots of the funeral cortege were shown, one car turns in another direction and everything else follows it. The driver was oblivious to the dozen or so cars following him until he glanced in his rear view mirror and realised what had happened. He tried to lose the cars following behind, but despite increasing his speed, they stuck with him. Eventually, he stopped to ask the other drivers why they were following him and they told him they'd been instructed to follow whichever car was in front of them. It was a disaster and he knew it'd be in his best interests if he

helped everyone find the cenotaph – a good decision considering some of the people who were none-too-pleased at the unnecessary diversion. He ended up getting there before we did!

I was graveside at the burial and I could feel eyes menacingly looking at me wondering why a photographer was there, but all it took was a glance from Reggie and people knew I was there because he'd personally asked me to be. I was then asked to go to the wake to take a few more shots and I was the only photographer there. I then went away, processed the films, put my stamp on the back of the pictures and delivered them to Reggie who seemed really pleased.

The next day, I learned that a legendary East London gangster had been snorting cocaine off the coffin as a mark of respect and then sold the pictures to the News of the World for £20,000!

From there on, I began getting calls two or three times a week from Reggie asking me to turn girls into Page Three stars and various other tasks and I got into a situation whereby it was costing me quite a bit of money, including a batch of prints that were to be taken around various pubs and clubs and sold as signed, limited photographs of Reggie. I said, "Reggie, this is costing me a lot of money," and he seemed surprised that I had to pay anything.

"Well how much do you need?" he asked. I told him and a brown paper bag containing my expenses turned up at the door within a few hours!

My last contact with Reggie Kray came while I was working away in America. Reggie had been released from prison on compassionate grounds due to ill-health. He was taken to a hospital in Norwich and he wanted me to take the last picture, so to speak. I flew home and was stopped at customs for not declaring a coat I'd bought and was subsequently searched, thinking all the time that if Reggie passed away while I was delayed, it would be a disaster. Eventually, I got away and headed for Central London because his people had asked me to get some shirts, cuff-links and a tie. The final picture was meant to show Reggie free at last, so I then headed off to East Anglia and made it to Reggie's bedside. He had a drip in is finger and so couldn't get a shirt on anyway, as it turned out. He also had a drip in his nose, but I took the pictures and while I was looking through the lens, I could tell just by looking into his eyes, he was a powerful man and had been there, seen it and done it. He wanted to see the pictures as quickly as possible, so I drove back to London, developed them and drove back again. Reggie liked the images but said, "What are we going to do about the tube?" I said, "If we take the tube out of the picture, it'll be a fake and one thing you're not is a fake. Surely you want your last picture to be a true reflection of yourself." I also added that you didn't notice the tube initially, you were drawn in by the eyes, and then you noticed the tube. He agreed with the reasoning and then shook my hand. "The next time we'll meet, we'll be in a better place," he said. He'd found religion and was content and ready to pass on and a week later, he died.

The Krays

Planet Hollywood

The opening of the Planet Hollywood restaurants was the first time real A-list movie stars had come into our presence. Of course we saw them at film premieres and so on but they never interacted with the photographers other than the occasional gimmicky shot. So when Planet Hollywood opened in Central London – Bruce Willis, Arnold Schwarzenegger and Sylvester Stallone all flew over for the launch – but the likes of Demi Moore and Charlie Sheen came with them. All of a sudden we had these fantastic combinations of top film stars who were totally accessible and willing to do whatever was needed to help promote the restaurant. I got to attend openings in New York, Chicago, Aspen, Boston and Miami and they all had pre-launch parties where only triple A-list talent were invited and if you weren't a name of some kind, you didn't get in. I remember in Miami, Stallone held the pre-opening party in his house and Madonna was there amongst others and it was fantastic to get inside the inner-sanctum as it were. I'd wandered around his house trying to decide if the paintings on the wall were real Picasso's – and of course they were. I was in his kitchen when Patrick Swayze handed some photos to Stallone and said, "Take a look at my new baby." I thought that was cute, until I discovered he was showing him pictures of a new jet he'd recently bought!

There was another time I went along with Piers Morgan to an opening in Aspen, Colorado just before Christmas and it was a magical, fairytale experience with snow everywhere, fairy lights – the works. Each

Planet Hollywood

"Planet Hollywood opened up a whole new chapter for movie stars."

Planet Hollywood location had a star attached to it and Aspen's was Don Johnson, who was dating Melanie Griffiths at the time and we ended up at a party having snowball fights in the grounds with Piers, Don and Melanie. The pictures were syndicated around the world and Piers later said, "I knew I'd made it when I was flying home on Rupert Murdoch's private jet, opening a copy of an american tabloid and seeing one of the pictures I'd had taken during the trip and was reading a caption that said 'Don Johnson and Melanie Griffiths having a playful snowball fight with Piers Morgan.'" That's the power of a picture because the general public didn't know that he'd only met them that day, but it certainly didn't do Piers' career any harm, did it?

Film stars hardly ever get to meet their fans because they'll go to the studio, get taken home and apart from the premieres, that'd be it – Planet Hollywood opened up a whole new chapter for movie stars and I think it's where the hysteria for movie stars really began because people knew certain actors would be at a certain place at a certain time.

Whenever you got the call for a Planet Hollywood launch, you'd be there. At the time, they had great parties, great food and, of course, great opportunities to meet and photograph the biggest names in the business.

Planet Hollywood

Oasis

Oasis have always been portrayed as the bad boys of rock, but when it actually comes down to it, I've always thought it's the women in their life who seem to rule the roost. If you play it the right way, you can usually get what you want from them, but it's invariably done by asking the females that surround them, be it girlfriends, wives or their mum.

There was one occasion at a Steve Coogan show – he was doing a live version of Alan Partridge – and Liam and Noel turned up with mum, Peggy. I asked her if she'd have a picture taken with her lads and she called them both over and they did what they were told. Of course, then you can break it down a bit and eventually you get the picture of the boys on their own, looking as usual like the Brothers Grimm.

I love their music and we need stars like the Gallaghers who have plenty of attitude and basically don't give a toss. They are few and far between these days.

Meg Matthews was a party animal and I always thought she was on the party circuit a little too much and eventually I think Noel just had enough of it. I was out in Las Vegas when they got married, though there were never any wedding pictures as such. At a party for one of Ronnie Wood's kids six months later, Meg turned up in what I can only describe as the wedding dress she probably never wore with flowers and lace all over. Noel was there in his leathers with his customary snarl and a bottle of Becks in his hand and they looked great together – it was the wedding picture the world had wanted, in many ways, though I don't think it was that long

Oasis

"Noel's a cool guy who does what he wants."

after that their relationship began to disintegrate.

Noel's a cool guy who does what he wants – he plays the game, but only plays occasionally.

Liam got together with Nicole Appleton after splitting with Patsy Kensit and he can never resist doing something in front of the camera, whether it's sticking his tongue out or giving you the V-sign, but my favourite picture of him was when he turned up to a Sunday morning premiere of the Sponge Bob Square Pants movie! He came over and asked if I'd take a picture of him with Sponge Bob and after realising he was serious, I took a few frames for him. He told me, "I never miss it – it's my favourite show and I watch it all the time with my son. It's got so many hidden meanings." So much for Mr Obnoxious!

Dominic Mohan, the former editor of Bizarre was really into Oasis and we went to Japan with them on one occasion. He knew his stuff and they knew he knew it, too, but you still had to be on your guard when Liam was around. They came into the bar where we were and started chatting and we'd been having a normal conversation when Liam decided it was time to throw drinks over us before he went to bed. I always felt he was testing people out to see if they'd kick off and he couldn't just leave the bar and go to bed – where is the rock and roll in that? He had to do something, but that's Liam Gallagher for you.

There was another time when I went over to cover them on tour as U2's support act in America. They had banned British photographers from having access on the tour so I called in a couple of favours

Oasis

ACCESS **ALL** AREAS

and went along representing Newsweek. America didn't care for Oasis because nobody knew who they were and so none of the photographers who were there were taking any pictures of them. They'd use the support act to focus their cameras and photograph various banners in the crowd. Noel and Liam were doing their stuff on stage and I was the only one who was interested – this was really pissing the lads off because they weren't used to playing second fiddle to anyone. Suddenly, Liam spots me in the pit, points at me, walks over and sticks his tongue out at my camera, all because I was the only one who could be bothered. He has a certain swagger and defiance on stage, but he doesn't do that much so there's only so many pictures you can take of him during a concert.

When the new line-up was announced, Noel decided he wanted to meet us in Starbucks! He's a clever guy and he gets his message over with a minimum of fuss and I've got a lot of respect for him.

Oasis

59

James Bond

I love James Bond for a number of reasons and my personal favourite Bond has to be Pierce Brosnan. He is the ultimate Bond and he lived the part while he was 007. I did a set of pictures that I am very, very proud of. I was invited on to the set of 'Tomorrow Never Dies' with Andy Coulson to film one particular stunt that the producers were keen to be used to help promote the new film. Filmed in Germany, there was a scene where a car is driving up a multi-story car park and it flies off the roof of the building and goes straight through an Avis car rental window opposite. I had to get it absolutely spot-on – and I could have easily f****d it up, because I don't normally do stuff like that. I knew I wouldn't get another chance, but managed to bag it exactly how I'd wanted it. Film shoots involving Bond are never less than exciting, trust me! The stunts were incredible and it began with a BMW-7 Series being fired out of a cannon off the back of a transporter and it smashed through the Avis shop front before resting in front of a desk. The pictures were on the front page of The Sun the next day and everyone was happy.

On that particular job, Pierce told us how he'd been injured the day before during a fight sequence and it had resulted in a nasty wound on his mouth. Stopping filming wasn't an option so they'd stitched him from the inside of his mouth and covered the cut that had been visible on the outside with make-up.

There was another time Pierce was showing off his 007 Omega watch on set and he was showing

James Bond

us it when he mentioned he had a spare one. Ian West, a friend of mine who works for PA Photo's shouted, "It's my birthday today! It's my birthday today!" and Pierce walked over and asked if it really was or not. Ian got out his driving licence to prove it was and Pierce handed him the £6,000 watch and said, "Well here's your birthday present." Such class!

It's great being privy to these inside secrets at the time, but things have tightened up a little in recent years and, dare I say have become a little less thrilling.

Roger Moore was a class act and never one to be ushered into doing something he didn't want to do. There was one occasion when The Sun were keen to promote their bingo cards and I had to ask every celebrity I was photographing if they'd pose with a bingo card for an additional shot. Some did – it would guarantee their picture in the paper if they did, but some didn't because, frankly, they didn't have to. I ducked out of a photo shoot with Roger Moore on location because I knew I'd have to ask him to hold a bingo card and I knew what his reaction would be. So Steve Lewis, another Sun photographer, went along and at the end, he passed the card to Moore who looked as though he was being handed a dead rodent. He said, "I won't be doing that and I shall now be adding a bottle of the hotel's finest claret to your room bill later on."

Another personal favourite shoot connected to Bond was when I took a set of pictures of the

James Bond

"Whatever Daniel Craig did, it was going to be a tough act following Pierce."

amazing Tina Turner, a consummate professional who looks fantastic and is a joy to work with. She was promoting her single, the theme to 'Goldeneye' and I managed to get the real gun James Bond used in the movie from the props department and the end result is stunning. She's a legend and I have to admit, I love her!

Whatever Daniel Craig did, it was going to be a tough act following Pierce. After he was unveiled as the new 007, there was an outcry that he was blond and then they said he was too short – the poor bloke couldn't win. Daniel just kept his mouth shut and got on with it but even the much-anticipated promotion for 'Casino Royale' ran into problems when his speedboat ride along the Thames had James Bond, complete with the life jacket that health and safety had made him wear – it wasn't his choice, but he still got a kicking for it. Compared with Bond photo shoots from the past, it was all a bit tepid with no stunts or visual feasts such as a car smashing into something – it's all a bit controlled now, but who knows? Maybe things will go back to the way they were for future movies – I hope so. Daniel's only answer was to deliver the goods in the movie, which in 'Casino Royale', I think he did and I think he'll win everybody over eventually.

James Bond

Chris Moyles

The first time I met Chris Moyles was in Ibiza. We'd gone out to cover the Radio 1 Roadshow with Zoe Ball and Chris was the early morning DJ at the time and hardly known at all. With that in mind, I had to make any picture I took of him interesting, so I got him to pose with various inflatable water wings, flippers and a snorkel – all the things he'd never do now, but when you're on your way up, you'll do whatever you have to. I have promised never to publish that photo and have been true to my word. The actual picture that got used instead was of Norman Cook and Zoe Ball on a lilo together – they'd just met, had hooked up and later got married.

Chris paid his dues on the graveyard shift to become the self-titled Saviour of Radio 1 and he's got the listening figures to back up his lofty claims. He's a cheeky chappy who has a laugh, enjoys himself and knows what his listeners want. He's surrounded himself with people who help keep his feet on the ground and I guess if he ever steps over the mark, they rein him back in.

I was with Chris in Hunstanton after a Radio 1 road show a few years back and we were all having a drink in the hotel bar in the evening. Suddenly, a kid of about 16 burst in shouting that his mate was being beaten up and he needed help. Chris was the first to get up and jumped over the wall and followed this kid without even thinking about what might lie in store leaving a few of us trailing behind. I later found out he got a bravery award for that, not that he told anyone, so there's another side to Chris Moyles that people perhaps don't know about. He obviously

Chris Moyles

> # "Chris paid his dues on the graveyard shift to become the self-titled Saviour of Radio 1."

cares about other people and whereas others who were as famous as he is might have hidden behind their security or whatever, he seems to be the kind of guy who isn't afraid of getting his hands dirty from time to time. It's not hard to see why he's turned out well because you couldn't meet a more down-to-earth couple than Chris' parents, who are the proudest people I think I've ever met. I think his family are the most important people in his life and I like that.

Chris Moyles

Best of the Caners

I took a picture of Sarah Harding downing a bottle of Drambuie at the NME Awards in 2007 which proved to be somewhat controversial. Here's this pretty Girls Aloud singer showing she could drink the Kaiser Chiefs under the table, but what it probably highlighted was how the culture of binge-drinking is prevalent in the UK more than anything else.

The most obnoxious person I've ever photographed is Paris Hilton. She cancelled three times before we finally pinned her down at a hotel for a few quick shots. Her people said she would be late, but I wasn't going anywhere and waited for her. When she finally turned up with her entourage she totally ignored me and went over and stood in front of a mirror, staring at herself for about five minutes – how shallow is that? We finally managed to get her to pose and she kept complaining about how tired she was and each flash that went off she'd go, "Ooh! My eyes, my eyes! Do I have to do this?" I took about 15 shots and she looked good, but boy, is she ever high maintenance.

Charlotte Church had been paid a serious amount of money by Orange to promote something or other and she turned up for a 9am cover shoot completely partied out having been out till 5am in the morning. Most people would have called up and cancelled, but she obviously wanted the money and went ahead with it. She was constantly belching throughout the shoot and apologised continually about being hung over, but she still looked fantastic and was good company. She could probably out-drink most rugby players, but she always delivers

Best of the Caners

the goods and I love her for that.

What can you say about a talent like Amy Winehouse? A flawed genius, the last time I photographed Amy was at the 2008 MTV awards where Amy was sat on Blake's knee and they looked totally loved-up. It's so sad to see one of our greatest singers for years seemingly spiralling out of control.

Pete Doherty looks like the great unwashed and again, you wonder what Kate Moss saw in him. You can't help but wonder where it all might end for both Pete and Amy – I hope it's a happy ending, but the signs weren't good at the time of writing.

Best of the Caners

Live Aid & Sir Bob

After Band Aid released 'Do They Know it's Christmas?' came Live Aid and July 13th, 1985 is a day neither myself nor millions of others will ever forget. I received a call out of the blue from LD Publicity asking whether I was interested in being one of the official photographers for a project involving Bob Geldof called Live Aid. I was told I'd get Access All Areas with all profits from the pictures going to charity. There would be six photographers including David Bailey and it turned out to be one of the best days of my life, completely unforgettable and a complete honour. It was a hot summer's day at a packed Wembley Stadium and it was artist after artist after artist – it never seemed to end and I thought I'd died and gone to heaven! It was a dream job and I doubt it will ever be topped.

I had 13 cameras that day – not all round my neck, of course – and I have so many wonderful memories, many of which I captured on film and my favourite shots are here, spread over the next few pages.

I was also working for Newsweek that day and the first two rolls of film I filled were taken by a courier who then went to Heathrow, hopped onto Concorde and flew to New York to hand deliver them to Newsweek's picture desk in person in time for their deadline – and they didn't even use the pictures in the end! Technology has come a long way since then, but that's how things had to be done.

I had to mark on each camera who exactly it was I was taking pictures for. Some were for a book on the event, some the Sundays and so on. The

Live Aid & Sir Bob

pictures were destined for all corners of the world and it was quite a job to keep everyone happy.

It was the greatest party atmosphere I've ever experienced. I managed to get a shot of Princess Diana, sat in the Royal Box with Prince Charles, David Bowie and several other people and it's clear she's lost in the music while everyone else is chatting around her. Perfect.

The Police, Paul McCartney, Alison Moyet, Paul Young, George Michael and Elton John – the list is endless and of course there was that moment when U2 came on and Bono went down into the crowd and couldn't get back up on to the stage again. This was their big moment and in later years he admitted he thought he'd f****d everything up – but of course he hadn't – and U2 went global after that day and for me, stole the show. The band admitted that they were totally pissed off with Bono at the time because there was only so long they could play the same chord for but, of course, in hindsight it was an iconic moment that everyone remembers.

Because we were working for the artists and the charity, nobody said no to anything we asked – we were all working for the same cause and that lowered all barriers. Egos were checked in at the door and we were all on a level playing field – no them and us scenarios – and that's why working for good causes is great for all concerned.

There were moments when a hush fell that was, in itself, deafening, and the video that accompanies The Cars singing 'Drive' was one such example.

Live Aid & Sir Bob

ACCESS
ALL
AREAS

Everybody was silent and just watched and the message hit home like a missile – that's why we were all there working for nothing – that's why the greatest names in music had come together for the day and those were the people we were doing it for. It wasn't about the music; it was about saving starving kids. It was perfect and the kick up the backside that the world needed and Bob Geldof pulled it altogether and he helped change the world – and good luck to him.

At the end of the day, I was more tired than I'd ever been in my life, but I was on an incredible high, too. Seeing Queen from such a privileged position perform 'Radio Ga Ga' will stay in my memory forever and I think if they were asked to name one moment that has stayed with them people would say it was the great Freddie Mercury, one of the greatest showmen this country has ever or will ever – produce, leading the crowd during that song.

Another favourite picture was back stage when, at the end of the night, Bob Geldof and Paula Yates were cuddling up. You could see the pride on her face and Bob is totally exhausted, but he'd done it and he does it so well. "F**k the address let's get the numbers!", as Sir Bob says.

Live Aid & Sir Bob

"Bob Geldof pulled it altogether and he helped change the world."

ACCESS **ALL** AREAS

ACCESS ALL AREAS

I first met Bob Geldof during his Boomtown Rats days and back then he was no more than a scruffy pop star that I photographed occasionally and that was about it. Then, of course, Live Aid came along and Bob, Bernard Docherty and Harvey Goldsmith offered me the opportunity of being one of six official photographers for the event with Access All Area passes that meant we could do pretty much anything we wanted.

Whatever pictures we took would all be owned by Live Aid and all profits would go back to the charity, which made perfect sense. Of course, we all jumped at the opportunity because this was perhaps the first occasion that we'd been given the chance to mingle with showbiz royalty safe in the knowledge that all the artists on the day would be happy to co-operate with us and let us get on with our jobs while they got on with theirs – in short, it was the chance of a lifetime.

The passes allowed us to go everywhere except the dressing rooms – which wasn't a problem because nobody really used them on the day. It was then that I really saw and realised what Bob was all about and that's basically having the ability to get people to do things they didn't want to do! He never bossed anyone around on the day, but kept things ticking along nicely, in-between going on TV to tell the nation to (cue heavy Northern Irish accent) "F**k the address let's get the numbers!" Priceless – but nobody minded because he was just showing his passion and the urgency of the situation in Africa in a way nobody had ever done before.

Live Aid & Sir Bob

"He had a way of communicating directly with the man on the street."

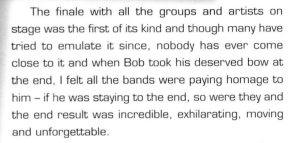

The finale with all the groups and artists on stage was the first of its kind and though many have tried to emulate it since, nobody has ever come close to it and when Bob took his deserved bow at the end, I felt all the bands were paying homage to him – if he was staying to the end, so were they and the end result was incredible, exhilarating, moving and unforgettable.

His wife Paula Yates was with him throughout the day and I took some beautiful images of them together at the end of the day, exhausted, virtually asleep but very much in love and I imagine their kids treasure those pictures.

Since then, it kind of became clear that though Bob had found fame through his music and done reasonably well, his true calling was waking people up to human catastrophes that were taking place in Africa and other parts of the world. He had a way of communicating directly with the man on the street as well as multi-millionaires and being able to organise the seemingly impossible.

Bob has a presence about him and I've taken a number of family portraits of him over the years and one of my favourites is of Bob with his three daughters and Tiger Lily, the daughter of Paula Yates and Michael Hutchence – and that for me sums the guy up. Bob took Tiger Lily into his home and treated her as his own flesh and blood and though he must have found the separation with Paula incredibly painful, he never once dished the dirt or said anything derogatory about her because he obviously loved her dearly in his own way. He has

Live Aid & Sir Bob

"He turned up and the world's media turned up with him."

always maintained this wonderful dignity and, having been through a divorce myself, he must have the patience of a saint to conduct himself publicly the way he has.

Many people in this world say what they want to do or what they'd like to do, but Bono and Bob – Morecambe and Wise as I call them – just go out and do it. There is one story that sums Bob up perfectly. I had an exhibition a while back at Getty Images Gallery, focusing on 20 years since Live Aid and it cost the organisers a lot of money. They asked me if I could get somebody famous to open the event, or at least turn up on one of the preview evenings. It's very difficult to get celebrities to do anything unless there is something in it for them because they are always being asked to do stuff and simply don't have enough hours in the day to meet even a fraction of the requests they receive. I asked how they felt about Bob Geldof and, of course, they were delighted at the suggestion – all I had to do was get Bob to do it! I called him up and said, "Bob, I've never asked anybody for anything, but a lot of people have put a lot of money into this project – would you consider coming along to help promote it?"

He said, "Yep." I panicked and suddenly thought he must be fobbing me off, so as the day approached, I called him up and double-checked. He said, "Dave, I said I'd turn up so I'll turn up," then he hung up. He turned up and the world's media turned up with him – he'd cleverly arranged to use the exhibition as a backdrop to the various messages he

Live Aid & Sir Bob

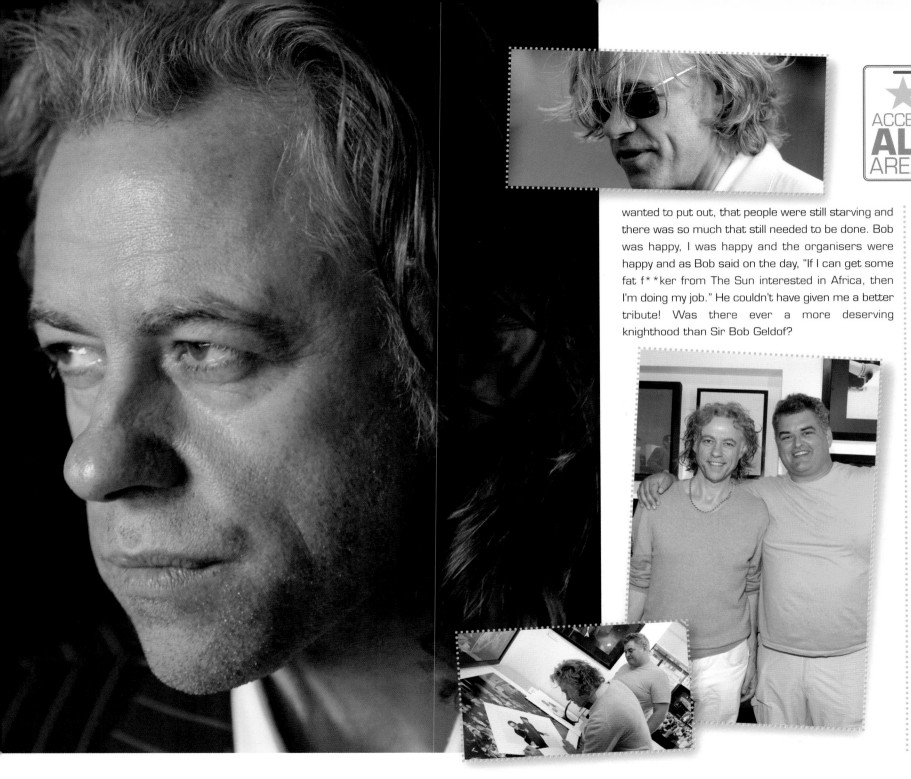

wanted to put out, that people were still starving and there was so much that still needed to be done. Bob was happy, I was happy and the organisers were happy and as Bob said on the day, "If I can get some fat f**ker from The Sun interested in Africa, then I'm doing my job." He couldn't have given me a better tribute! Was there ever a more deserving knighthood than Sir Bob Geldof?

Live Aid & Sir Bob

Band Aid 2

Before Live 8, there was Band Aid 2, which resulted in the modern version of 'Do They Know It's Christmas?' Recorded at Abbey Road Studios, the top stars of the day were there and I was in the recording booth shooting the stills as each singer took their turn. There was Justin Hawkins from The Darkness, Tom Chaplin from Keane, Sugababes and dozens of others. Damon Albarn from Blur had apparently asked to come along, though not to sing, just to make everyone cups of tea! It was surreal having the usually difficult Albarn walk up and ask, "You want sugar in that, Dave?" Getty Images agreed to give back every penny earned from the images taken that day to the Band Aid charity and because of that, nobody could say no to having their photograph taken – it had taken alot of sorting out, but between us we did it and in total there was £45,000 raised in royalties from selling those images around the world.

Bono couldn't make it in the morning and as the day progressed, every singer who went in to record the song tried to nick his famous "and tonight thank god it's them, instead of you," line. Robbie Williams tried, Justin Hawkins tried, but nobody came near to even threatening to beat the master.

Bono finally arrived about 10pm, by which time most people had gone home and I can only liken the ensuing photo session of Bob Geldof and Bono in the studio to a modern-day Morecambe and Wise sketch. They are like two big kids, fooling around constantly, but with great admiration for one another. Then Bono goes in and sings his version of

Band Aid 2

the song and nails it in one go.

Some people said the end result wasn't as good as the original, but it was never about that – it was about getting people off their arse and making them aware again. When Bono and Geldof start something, everyone else follows and things happen and Live 8 followed on from Band Aid 2 and yet more millions were raised for the people of Africa, in turn saving millions of lives. It's all about stars checking in their egos at the door and getting on with it, which on this occasion, they most certainly did and it was a genuine honour to have been involved.

Band Aid 2

Live 8

After the recording of Band Aid 2, there was great demand to recreate the Live Aid concert and Bizarre editor at the time, Dominic Mohan, was hugely instrumental in driving the dream forward, even though Bob Geldof himself initially believed it would never happen. Dominic called up several bands and all of them were up for it and then things really gathered momentum from there. Of course, when Geldof and Bono threw their weight back behind it, it was no longer a case of 'if', just 'when'. Held before hundreds of thousands in Hyde Park, Live 8's line-up surpassed Live Aid as far as I was concerned, partly because there were some fantastic combinations of acts on the day itself.

There was U2 and Paul McCartney playing together, Elton John and Pete Doherty plus the likes of Coldplay, Madonna, Robbie Williams and Pink Floyd, who hadn't played live together for god knows how long. Geldof bullied more bands into saying yes in his own inimitable way – and would you want to turn Sir Bob down if he called up? Even The Who reformed for the concert and I was there with my triple A pass to record it all on yet another unforgettable day in the life of a celebrity photographer. Here is a selection of my favourite moments from this most historic occasion with my favourite being the moment when Madonna brought on stage Birhan Weldu, former victim of the Ethiopian famine whose picture had touched so many at the original Live Aid concert 20 years earlier. Birhan was now a beautiful young woman and if that didn't drive the message home about

Live 8

"Live 8 was, and remains a brilliant moment but what is more important is the brilliant movement of which it was a part. This gives the poorest of the poor real political muscle for the first time. It is this movement of church people and trade unionists, soccer moms and student activists, that will carry the spirit of Live 8 on. This movement, not rock stars, will make it untenable in the future to break promises to the most vulnerable people on this planet. That was always why we put on the concerts." **Bono**

what the whole concert was all about, nothing would. The reception was incredible and she was a little bemused by all the attention – all she wanted to do was ride on the London Underground! Fantastic!

Live 8

Live 8

ACCESS **ALL** AREAS

Live 8

ACCESS **ALL** AREAS

Diana

Diana

Probably the most photographed women in the world in recent times. Much loved and much missed!

Prince William and Harry at The Diana Tribute Concert. Ballet was one of Diana's favourite events to watch.

Diana

46664
The Nelson Mandela Concert

I went over to South Africa to cover the 46664 concert held at Green Point Stadium, Cape Town. It was hosted by Nelson Mandela with the aim of raising awareness of the spread of HIV and AIDS in South Africa. Bono, Bob Geldof, Beyonce and Annie Lennox were some of the musicians who had agreed to appear and it turned out to be an amazing project that changed my life on so many different levels.

Being taken to Robben Island, where Nelson Mandela (whose prison number was 46664) had been incarcerated for 25 years of his life and taking pictures of the great man outside his prison cell was a very poignant moment for everybody who was there – and I also shot some very strong images from inside the cell itself.

But my emotional rollercoaster really kicked in when I was invited to accompany Beyonce and Bono on to an orphanage in one of the poverty-stricken local townships. The only way I can describe the woman who ran this orphanage is that she reminded me of Old Mother Hubbard – and I say that with the utmost respect. It was called Rosie's Bopihina and it was basically a two up, two down dirt hut housing 45 orphaned kids. They hadn't a clue who Bono and Beyonce were and at one point, Bono picked up these two tiny babies called Hope and Charity and you could see he was just a concerned father like anyone else would be. Beyonce was very distressed by it all, as we all were, as we saw harrowing scenes of human despair and when kids are involved, it just seems to

46664

Hogie in Uganda, part of the Listen Project.

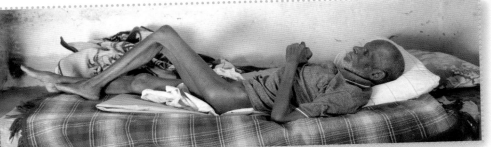

multiply the horror. In one room there were eight cots, most with three babies crammed in top-to-tail and though they all looked as though they'd been fed and looked after, it was incredibly hard to witness.

At one point, Bono sat down and explained the whole AIDS situation in Africa and how whole generations of people aged 30 to 40 have been wiped out because of the virus. Most of the kids were being brought up by their elderly grandparents who were just getting on with things as best they could.

The lack of funding from governments and various agencies meant that mothers were passing the virus on to their unborn child despite the fact that one anti-viral injection during delivery would give the child a very good chance of not contracting AIDS from their mother. The injection cost no more than $4 – yet still nobody was doing anything about it.

Bono knows that when he beats the drum, people sit up and take notice and he will never let causes such as this go. He knows the hard facts and spreads the word with great passion and energy and it changed my life in many ways because that visit made me sit up and take notice, probably for the first time. While we were there, there was a knock at the door. It was someone bringing another baby to the orphanage because there was nobody who could look after it and, despite there being seemingly no room left, they took the infant in – because that's what they do. This was the last stop for these kids because there was nowhere left to go and to see all this actually happen in front of your own eyes was heartbreaking.

It was surreal in many ways and I was taking pictures of these little babies, most with sadness and pain in their eyes, when all I'd been used to was taking fluffy showbiz shots of the mega rich and famous. I knew my life would never be the same again and that I had to do something to help.

They told us that there were two babies in the back who had died, but they couldn't afford to bury them and Beyonce and her mum were in floods of tears, people were digging in their pockets to find money, but of course, there was no quick-fix solution for a problem of such magnitude. I know Bono later took his whole family back – without the cameras, because personal publicity is not why he does what he does – I'm not sure Beyonce has been back because I doubt if she could cope with it again.

As the visit drew to a close, Bono and Beyonce were taken back to the city and I stayed on for a while. Somebody commented that it was all well and good taking all these pictures but they still had nothing to eat. They had cabbages, but nothing else for that evening so I asked my driver, Lukman if there was a market or something where I could go and buy some provisions for these people. I called my wife and told her I wanted to stay on for a while and actually do something and she didn't object. For once in my life, I wanted to be involved with something other than making money – I'd never done that before, but it wasn't a whim just to make myself feel better about the lifestyle I would return to in London, it was an urge to give back – I had to do something.

46664

We drove to a local market and Lukman , a very dignified and proud man, told me the things that would be desperately needed back at the orphanage. He said that they needed wheat, maize, cooking oil and milk substitute, so we piled sacks and boxes up on a cart. This big pile of food cost just £250 – the price of a posh meal for two in London. We took the food back to Rosie's and I told the staff it was a donation from all the press who were out there for the Mandela concert. Their reaction was unbelievable and they cried, sang and danced. It was incredible and they told me they wouldn't have to worry about food now for six months and at that moment, I understood why people like Bono and Bob Geldof do what they do – it's addictive for all the right reasons and I was honoured to be able to help those wonderful people, even in just a small way.

My life changed from that day and I wanted to become more actively involved in doing whatever I could do to help. I spoke with a woman called Patricia Heigham, who used to be a researcher for Hunter S. Thompson. She asked me if I really wanted to see things and whether I really wanted to become involved. I think she could see I was serious so she took me to a place called Umtata, where she was working on a project called African Solutions For African Problems, which is all about helping African people help themselves through education and by helping them eat and learn about things like water irrigation. It was December by this point so I decided to organise a Christmas party for the local orphanage and started going around

46664

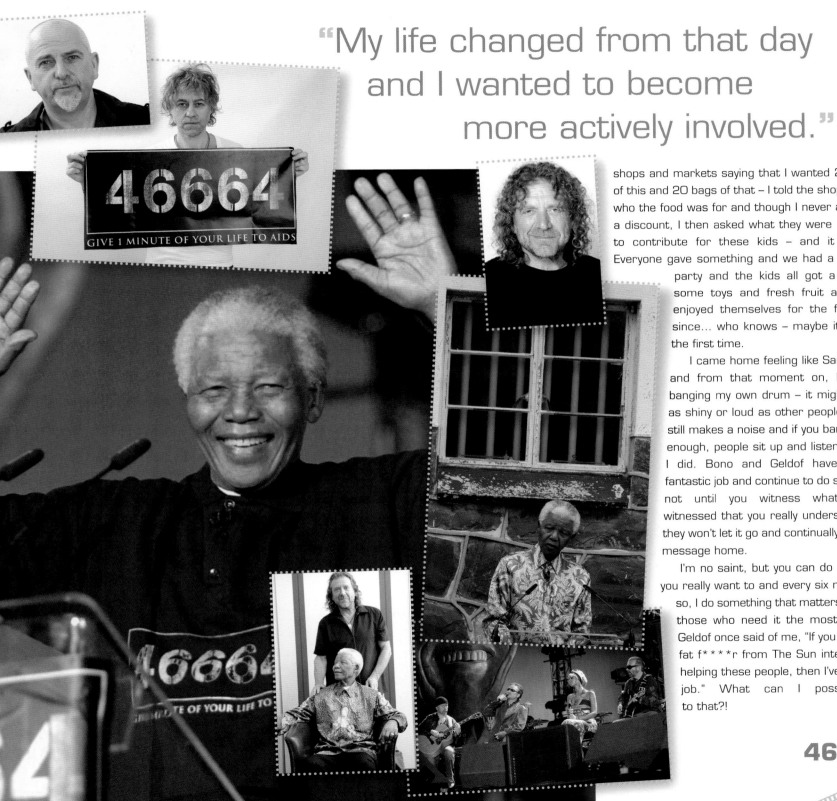

"My life changed from that day and I wanted to become more actively involved."

shops and markets saying that I wanted 20 boxes of this and 20 bags of that – I told the shopkeepers who the food was for and though I never asked for a discount, I then asked what they were prepared to contribute for these kids – and it worked. Everyone gave something and we had a fantastic party and the kids all got a cracker, some toys and fresh fruit and really enjoyed themselves for the first time since... who knows – maybe it was for the first time.

I came home feeling like Santa Claus and from that moment on, I've been banging my own drum – it might not be as shiny or loud as other people's, but it still makes a noise and if you bang it hard enough, people sit up and listen, just like I did. Bono and Geldof have done a fantastic job and continue to do so, but it's not until you witness what they've witnessed that you really understand why they won't let it go and continually drive the message home.

I'm no saint, but you can do your bit if you really want to and every six months or so, I do something that matters and help those who need it the most. As Bob Geldof once said of me, "If you get some fat f****r from The Sun interested in helping these people, then I've done my job." What can I possibly say to that?!

46664

ACCESS **ALL** AREAS

Mandela
90th Birthday Dinner & Concert

Mandela

A host of stars and celebrities visited London to attend the 90th birthday celebrations of Nelson Mandela in June 2008.

NELSON MANDELA AT 90

Mandela

Bono & U2

I've been fortunate to work with some of the biggest names in music and show business over the past 30 years or so, but my all-time hero is without doubt Bono. Being at close quarters the day he went into the crowd and picked out a girl at Live Aid and being present and able to photograph that particular moment as it happened still sends a tingle down my spine 20 years later.

I first met Bono on a Sunday morning in 1984 prior to the recording of Band Aid's original 'Do They Know It's Christmas?' I was already a huge fan of U2 by that time and this is a hard business to be in if you are totally smitten with the people you are photographing. It shifts the goalposts somewhat and you see things through different eyes and I've been in rooms where previously unflappable people have turned to jelly and have become a jabbering wreck when their hero walked into the room. It's difficult sometimes, but I've been able to be professional enough to get past that and have never had the urge to go up to Bono and say, "I love you Mr Bono and I love your music," like some awe-struck teenage girl! Not yet, anyway!

To be in the photographers' pit, however, when U2 blaze out something like 'Sunday, Bloody Sunday' in front of 100,000 people – while you join in by singing at the top of your voice – is something very special and makes me feel very privileged – it doesn't get much better than that, believe me.

I've worked with RMP, U2's PR company, for many years and they'll call up and invite me to certain events and occasions. I've been over to

Bono & U2

"I was already a huge fan of U2 by that time."

America with the band on tour and have taken some memorable images over the years such as Bono coming out on stage in his muscle-man suit posing to the crowd – he's always had a great interaction with his fans, as you can see by the pictures I've selected in these few pages.

Bono never worries about his own personal safety and it must be a nightmare for security teams at U2 gigs because he wants to get right in there amongst his fans. I remember him crowd surfing at the Astoria one time and took a picture of Jerry Judge, one of the best security guys in the world, desperately holding on to Bono's feet before he disappeared into a sweaty mass of people at the front of the stage – was Bono worried? Never – he loved every minute of it because he's a genuine rock god.

There was one very poignant image of Bono taken within a few hours of his father dying that still stirs the emotions. I know his dad had been very ill, but he must have figured the best therapy at that moment in time was to go ahead with the concert and share his grief with his fans. As he spoke, you could see the tears in his eyes and at one point he just lay down on the stage, immersed in the moment. It was a fantastic tribute to his father from a very passionate man.

There was one occasion, however, when I completely blew a fuse at Bono and I ended up shouting and screaming at him and when Hogie loses it, which is rare, people tend to realise I'm not the happiest of bunnies. There was a Greenpeace demonstration taking place at Sellafield following a concert in Manchester back in 1992. U2 were planning their own protest until the police warned everyone that if they turned up, they'd be arrested. It seemed as though it had been called off and so we all ended up having a drink and a bit of a party back at the hotel. I went over to Bono and the band who confirmed it was not going to happen, so I decided I'd had enough and set off to drive back to London. As I went outside, somebody with inside info then came up and said, "It's not off, it's going to happen – they just had to tell you it was off so that everyone could hear." I said I'd drive up to Sellafield and left my number so they could call me if and when the protest began.

I was asleep in my car when I was awoken by a policeman saying, "You're missing it mate! It's happening round the back." I asked what he meant and he told me that Bono and the band were coming up the estuary in an inflatable dinghy to land on the sandbanks outside the nuclear plant. I couldn't believe it and started driving round like a madman until I found the car park where they'd all met up, just in time to see Bono and company walking up the beach. A photographer from The Mirror, who was married to one of the PR people connected to U2 was there – but I wasn't because someone had forgotten to call me. I walked towards them, ranting and raving. "You bastards! I've been asleep in my car waiting for this and nobody called me…" They tried to calm me down and asked what it was I wanted so I asked them to get their gear back on and go back to the sandbanks – which they

Bono & U2

did! I think they could see I was completely pissed off and thought the best solution would be to comply on this occasion. I got my shot, the Mirror guy shared a few negatives with me and the world was all good again.

My wife Janice was making a documentary about Live Aid – 20 Years On and U2 drummer Larry and Bono met us in central London and there was one point during the interview when my wife asked Bono a particular question and he just started to cry and asked for the filming to be stopped. He told us that he'd gone to a moment in time where he didn't want to be. He went away, composed himself and apologised and we continued, but for me, that showed a glimpse of a man few people see, when the horrors he's witnessed are too much even for him

One of my favourite pictures was when I was stood behind Bono at Live 8, the concert organised two decades after Band Aid, as he walked out on the stage at Hyde Park and then travelled up to Murrayfield where he did the same thing and I was behind him again because if you get special access like that, you've got to take pictures nobody else is able to or else what's the point of being there?

I went over to Ireland in 2003 for the launch of Bono's charity book Peter and The Wolf that he'd illustrated and created with his two daughters. I met his wife, the lovely Ali Hewson and their girls, Jordan and Eve. He showed me his artwork for the book in his studio where we got some nice shots and there was another occasion when he posed for

Bono & U2

some fantastic pictures at his best friend Guggi's exhibition – Bono is very visual and he understands what makes a good picture so at various points he'd shout, "Photograph me now Dave!" and he'd pop his head up behind a giant egg cup or whatever.

Bono & U2

Boy George

Boy George was, in the Eighties, the modern-day Britney Spears – always interesting, never dull and always threatening to self-destruct. He never went anywhere without make-up and was a walking fashion statement and people like George are what makes my job so fascinating in that whatever trend is the flavour of the month, I'll go and photograph it. He would dress up as a Goth one day with his hair spiked up and make-up, a geisha girl the next and so on. It got to the stage where one of the most sought after pictures was trying to get George without any make-up on.

One afternoon, I got a call from Steve Strange telling me he was going shopping with George later in the day – that's how things work sometimes and he told me when and where they would be. As he came out of Brown's in South Malton Street, I raised my camera to get a couple of frames and George ran over to me and whacked me across the head with his yellow, frilly umbrella. It was one of my most humiliating experiences and George told me he'd "speak to me later" before waddling off with Strange. I got the picture and it made the front page of The Sun the next day, but I did wonder if I'd over-stepped the mark or not…

The next day, he called me up and told me to meet him at Heathrow. He said, "Look, my image is what I'm all about. I love being photographed by you, but just ask. If you ask, I'll always stop and pose for you." And since then he always has done – and I've always asked.

Some time after that, George's brother, David

Boy George

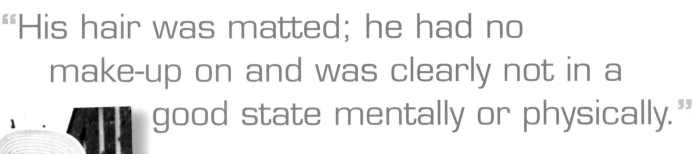

"His hair was matted; he had no make-up on and was clearly not in a good state mentally or physically."

ACCESS ALL AREAS

O'Dowd, a nice guy who was trying to get into pop photography, phoned me because he was genuinely concerned that his brother's life was in danger due to heroin abuse. I went along with Sun reporter Nick Ferrari who then wrote the story, 'George: Eight Weeks To Live', which blew the lid off his drug problems at the time and maybe saved his life. I got a call to go to North London where George was known to be staying and he passed me in another car as I drove towards the address. His hair was matted; he had no make-up on and was clearly not in a good state mentally or physically. We managed to follow him until he finally pulled over and spoke to Nick, but I didn't take any shots – if I had, people would have seen for themselves just what a perilous state George was in. He asked us to go to his house a couple of hours later where he'd give us an interview and pose for a couple of pictures. By the time we arrived, he was smartly dressed and looked immaculate, wearing white denim from head to toe, with a white cap and full make-up on. All over the jacket he was wearing was printed the words 'Men F**k Me Stupid'. I said, "George, I'll never get that in a family newspaper," and he told me I'd just have to try. I told him to work with me and somehow we managed to pull it off due to the angles we shot him at. It was the perfect image of a man in need of help and also one of my favourite pictures of George because even

at his lowest, he was still professional and wanted to maintain his public image. Shortly after this, he went into rehab having publicly admitted he was a drug addict and I think that's why, thankfully, one of Britain's most influential and genuine pop stars is still around today.

Boy George

The Rolling Stones

I first shot the Rolling Stones at Wembley in 1980, which was pretty run-of-the-mill-stuff, but not long after that, they played The 100 Club, which is literally just a small, claustrophobic room in London and it was there I managed to get some fantastic pictures of Mick Jagger, stripped to the waste, strutting his stuff. It was real, in-your-face stuff and it was the sort of situation where, if you loved the Stones, you felt like you had died and gone to heaven. Jagger was a lean, mean fighting machine and even to this day, he moves around the stage more than any other artist around. He never stops running from one side of the stage to the other – he is a true legend in every sense of the word.

When the Stones hit town, they completely take over – I've seen them virtually rent out the whole of The Four Seasons Hotel in London, with everyone connected to them having their own suite. They all have their own managers and you have to keep everyone happy and there's a lot of juggling to be done because without Mick Jagger and Keith Richards, there is no Rolling Stones – they are the essence and heartbeat of the band.

My favourite picture of the band is where they are all dressed up as gangsters, shot at The 100 Club in February 1986. We weren't allowed in, but they did agree to do a picture for us when they came off stage after performing a tribute gig for Ian Stewart, an original founder member of the band, known as the 'fifth Rolling Stone', who had died two months earlier.

It was a freezing cold night and when the doors

The Rolling Stones

"They played the 100 Club, which is literally just a small, claustrophobic room in London."

ACCESS
★
ALL
AREAS

GET BACK IN YER PRAM, WHAM!

Jagger gives Andy a piece of lip

The Rolling Stones

The Rolling Stones

"Mick likes to play with the press."

were opened for us to come in and get a quick picture, all our lenses steamed up because it was so hot and sweaty inside and nobody could see what they were taking shots of! I tried to clear my lens with a chamois leather and managed to get an image of them that looks as though they are in some speakeasy bar in Chicago – absolutely fantastic!

I've shot pictures of the Stones' kids over the years, too. I was at the Christening of Georgia May where we'd done a deal with Mick's spokesman that if we kept a respectable distance, they'd come out of the church and pose for the photographers on the steps.

At the premiere of 'Shine A Light', the Martin Scorsese documentary on the band, a Jack Sparrow-like Keith Richards looked like he was going to fall over at any moment whereas Jagger is more of a dignified statesman. Mick isn't a rock star god when he's not on tour – I remember we were waiting for him at some family get-together and he turned up by coming to the location from an unexpected angle. He tapped me on the shoulder and said, "Missed me!" before going inside – it's like a game with him and one that a lot of the celebrities regularly play. Mick doesn't go around London with bodyguards – he travels around on his own and does his own thing and by doing so he attracts less attention because of it. Mick reckons that by the time somebody recognises him, he's moved on and in that respect, he leads a relatively normal life.

On tour, it's a different matter and Mick likes to play with the press. I went to Japan with Piers

The Rolling Stones

Morgan because we'd convinced The Sun editor that this was going to be the tour to end all tours. Phil Collins and Paul McCartney were both in Japan, too, so it made perfect sense to be out there. We arrived, suitably jet-lagged and got our press passes for the concert. I was the only photographer who was shooting the gig, but as I went to shoot Mick at one corner of the stage, he'd run over to the other side. When I walked over to the other side, he'd run back again. He was toying with me and just letting me know he was in control. After a while, I took my seat with Piers, about five rows back, and within half-an-hour, we were both fast asleep as our jet-lag kicked in.

We were staying at the Osaka Palace Hotel – a massive place with a north and a south wing and only really one way in and out of each side. I called up Mick's management because we needed a picture to go with the interview Piers was going to do. They asked when we were leaving and I told them 4pm that day and they agreed to sort out something, but as I ended up waiting at one entrance for him Mick would go out of the other, then I'd switch over and wait again and he'd return through the other entrance. In the end, I just thought, 'f**k this' and Piers and me left to go and interview Phil Collins instead – a jet-lagged Hogie is not to be messed with, I can assure you, no matter who I'm photographing.

A little while later, Mick called up Piers and asked why we'd left. He explained we'd had a bollocking from our editor because we hadn't got

The Rolling Stones

The Rolling Stones

The Rolling Stones

either an interview or a picture and to justify our large expenses bill, we needed a guaranteed interview, which Phil Collins had given us. Mick said, "Oh, I was going to do the interview this afternoon, too." It eventually transpired that Mick gave a much better interview than he probably would have done, partly because we'd pulled the rug and the balance had shifted slightly. I still didn't get the picture I wanted and had to go with live shots instead, but it was honours even on that occasion.

The Stones are always visually very interesting on stage and invariably do something unusual every time they play. For a photographer, they make fascinating subjects and I've a ton of great memories associated with the band and each member. I was invited out to Boston with a triple A pass and could shoot whatever I wanted, so long as

Liam and Noel would have trouble trying to keep up with me and Keith

EXCLUSIVE by Victoria Newton

RONNIE WOOD ON THE STONES AND THE STOUT

The Rolling Stones

IT'S ONLY ROCK 'N OLD

their management approved them first. I sat there watching Mick on the PlayStation or various arcade games back stage and you'd have to see the gear they take with them around the world in person to actually believe it. They do their best to take their home lives on the road with them and have as many home comforts as possible. Snooker table, chefs and family members and friends – they're all there wherever they go because, as Mick said, this is their life and if they're touring for 18 months, they tour in style with a minimum of disruption. They've surrounded themselves with fantastic people, all the best in their field and that's why they are still the greatest rock and roll band in the world and when they stop touring, they go off and do their own thing. They know what they want and enjoy their lifestyle to the max – they are four very sophisticated guys – living legends in fact.

The Rolling Stones

ACCESS **ALL** AREAS

The Rolling Stones

Elton John
Tantrums and Tiaras

I first met Elton John in the early eighties and I suppose he was a forerunner for Boy George in many ways. Every time he went on stage he'd wear a different hat, a different outfit or whatever and you'd get a great set of pictures. His glasses were wacky, he'd wear Liberace-style clothes or military gear, dance around on his piano – he'd always do something because he was the master showman of the time.

I suppose I missed the early outrageous years during the seventies and as he grew older, he became a little more conservative, but luckily, it wasn't until he'd given us a couple of decades worth of being extrovert in one form or another.

There was one occasion when we had to go that extra mile to impress Elton in order to get something a little different. David Furnish, Elton's partner, was having a fiftieth birthday party in London and Bizarre editor, Andy Coulson, came up with the idea of hiring a horse-drawn carriage and dressing up as a couple of royal footmen. It was worth a try, so we did it and arrived at Elton's home, carrying a huge birthday cake. We were invited in and though Elton wasn't quite ready, David was there and he couldn't stop laughing because we'd gone to so much trouble. Elton popped down to see what was going on and said if we waited until he'd finished his make-up, he'd come out and do a picture with the cake – and we ended up with a wonderful front page lead the following day.

Elton had problems with his huge period wig and couldn't actually get into the waiting car with it on,

Elton John

"I suppose I missed the early outrageous years during the seventies. "

so they had to deliver him to the party in the back of a furniture van sat on a throne – only Elton could get away with that! We turned up at the party with our horse-drawn cart, got into the venue with no problem whatsoever – well, you would, wouldn't you? – and got an exclusive front-row position as Elton and David arrived. It just goes to show that if

Elton John

107

ACCESS **ALL** AREAS

you're prepared to make that extra effort, more often than not, you'll be rewarded.

I've done loads of stuff with Elton over the years, but one of the most poignant was a picture I took of him performing a duet with Pete Doherty at Live 8. Elton came on stage, ever the professional looking fantastic and totally prepared, whilst Pete came on looking totally wasted and dishevelled. It all went horribly wrong and there was one picture after they'd finished their number and were leaving the stage and it captured Elton looking so disappointed with Pete,

Elton John

"He wants to grow old gracefully."

though he never actually said as much. He'd given him the chance on a world stage but Doherty had blown it and I think Elton had wanted to help him out because he genuinely cares about people.

Today, Elton is Mr Conservative, but he's been there and done it so if he wants to grow old gracefully, why not? He's had more colour in his life than most – and he's got the outfits to prove it.

Elton John

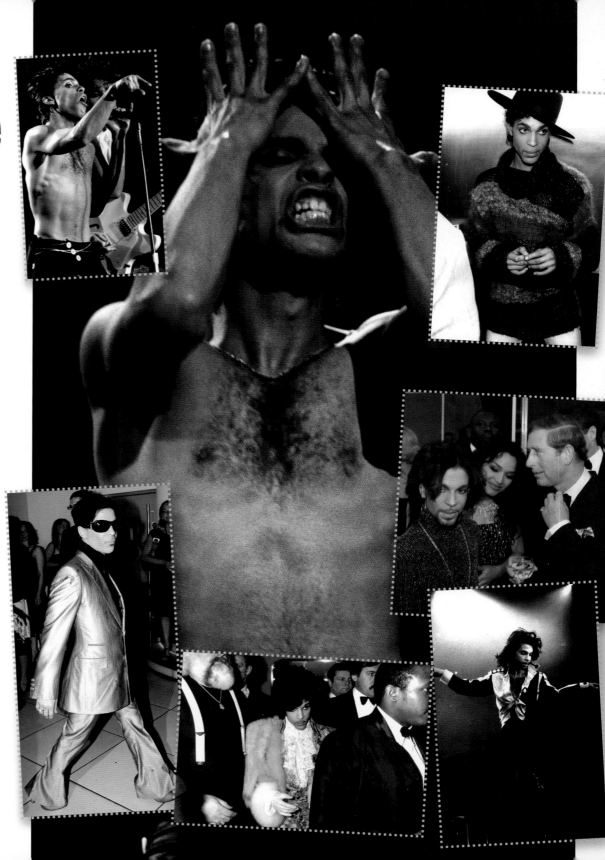

Prince

Prince was one of those artists who I think decided very early on in their careers that they were going to be difficult. He changed his name to a symbol – which no computer had, of course, so all written media needed to acquire the relevant software or call him 'The Artist Formerly Known As Prince' – it was ridiculous – but he used to get away with it because he was fantastic, massive and could do whatever he wanted – and therein lay the problem because when nobody says no to you or advises you that something might not be a good idea, usually born out of fear, it can be a case of the Emperor's got no clothes.

I've shot him on stage in Madison Square Garden wearing or using all kinds of various disguises and props and he'd never disappoint. The Sun's philosophy is all based around being the first and that means they want the first pictures of any new tour or concert – that's what it's all about and we don't wait for pictures to come to us, we go to them and make sure we do the job. For example, Prince was opening in Paris and several of us travelled over with the accreditation and passes we all needed only to be told on arrival by his people that there would be no photographers allowed. I said that they must be joking, but they insisted Prince didn't want to be photographed that day. In a situation like that, you either roll over and play dead or go to Plan B. I decided on the latter because I had a job to do and I wasn't going to take no for an answer. A few of us managed to sneak into the gig and I used to be the master of the

Prince

110

"He was constantly setting us challenges and he rarely granted total access."

stolen image. It was all a game in the eighties and if you got past security, it was all about waiting for the right moment before whipping your camera out and taking the shot you wanted. I'd then have to hide the film in my underpants or sock in case I was

rumbled or give it to a mate to take out of the venue. On this occasion, Prince was lowered on to the stage on a bed with a bevy of beauties surrounding him – it was a great scene, but we couldn't blow my cover too quickly, so I waited and waited and eventually I took out my camera and started to take a fabulous series of shots. At that point, I entered what I can only describe as tunnel vision whereby only you and the picture matters. That's when we were introduced to two of the biggest man-mountain security guards you're ever likely to meet! "Will you come with us please, sir?" I thought, 'shit!' I could see myself being thrown into a side street and searched until they found all the film, but Prince was far too subtle to endorse such heavy-handedness. He had a far more intelligent way of dealing with naughty photographers. We were taken back stage, had the cameras taken off us before being walked to the front row of the show where we were given a seat each, flanked by two security guards either side. It was more torturous than any physical punishment because he knew how much it would frustrate us, sat in the perfect position as fantastic opportunity after fantastic opportunity passed us by.

He was constantly setting us challenges and he rarely granted total access – it was often a case of 'see what you can get'. I was invited to his Paisley Park home in Minneapolis when he was due to launch a new album so I checked with his management that it was all definitely on for one last time before I flew out. It was a long way to go to get

told 'nothing doing', so after I'd got all the assurances it was all still on, I flew over and after checking into the hotel, I received a call telling me he'd changed his mind – there'd be no pictures. I lost it, I'm afraid, and explained that I wanted a picture for my troubles and that I wasn't interested in playing his ridiculous games. I told them they couldn't screw me or The Sun around and that I'd completely wasted my time and there'd be repercussions – after a while, they relented and allowed me to shoot the first three numbers of this most intimate gig at his house.

I was happy with that because that's why I'd gone over there in the first place. I got my stuff and went outside where Prince's limo was parked up. I told his driver that I was his official photographer and that he had to drive me into town so I could develop the pictures and then get them approved by the man himself – and he fell for it – and that's exactly what we did. Job done!

There was a period when he wasn't doing much at all and he just turned up unannounced at the Prince's Trust concert so I managed to get Prince Charles and Prince together for a picture and on this occasion, he came over and had a chat with us – he didn't have anything to promote so he wasn't this little arrogant prima donna anymore – nor was he flavour of the month at that point, either, so what would have been a fantastic picture a few years earlier, was largely ignored because there was a much better one I took of Prince Charles glancing at Liz Hurley's legs! Even Prince couldn't top that, I'm afraid.

Prince

Rock & Pop Legends

Freddie Mercury

Farrokh Bulsara, better known as Freddie Mercury, was a showman par excellence. One of the most colourful and entertaining guys I've had the pleasure of working with, Freddie's death left a void that's never really been filled. He was the greatest entertainer of his time and being present while Queen and Freddie performed 'Radio Ga Ga' at Live Aid will remain in my memory – and no doubt everyone else who witnessed it – forever. Freddie could conduct 100,000 people as if it were a school choir and get them to sing and clap in sync – not, I imagine quite as easy as he made it look.

Camp as hell and always flamboyant, he made a fascinating subject to photograph and people left a Freddie Mercury concert with big smiles on their faces – isn't that what this business is supposed to be about?

I remember a party he held at a roof garden in London and when I got into the lift there were all these naked people, all with body painted uniforms on and at the party there was a living sculpture – a glass tank with naked, painted, people in – you really had to see it to believe it. Page Three star of the day Sam Fox was at that party and Freddie, as gay as he was, loved women and wanted me to introduce him to Sam. He tried to get her to shake her boobs around and he was like a big kid, jumping up and down, but he was loads of fun to be around and he didn't care what people thought of him. At Rock in Rio he came on stage dressed as a woman with

false boobs, the lot – anything to be outrageous and that's what he was all about and the world is less colourful without him.

He partied hard, lived a life of decadence and excess and paid the ultimate price, but I think if he had the chance to do it all again, he probably wouldn't change a single thing.

Rock & Pop Legends

Michael Hutchence

Michael Hutchence was very much the archetypal rock god. I photographed him several times, including the time he went away for the weekend with Kylie Minogue on The Orient Express and the guy just oozed sex appeal and was born to be a star. Women adored him and guys respected him and he dated some amazing women including Paula Yates and the supermodel Helena Christensen. Friendly with everyone he had a rare ability to charm those around him with little effort, he seemed like a modern-day version of Jim Morrison.

I once went out to Spain to photograph him and INXS and after the gig he promised to come to a photo shoot the following morning. "I'm gonna go to bed early, get up and look great," he told me – but as he went to head back to his room for the night, one of his old pals from Australia turned up unannounced and he decided to have one drink with him… then another, and another – you can probably see where this is heading!

He was due to meet me at 9am the next day and he rolled up at 9.05am and said, "I've not been to bed yet." I looked at him and said, "Yeah, I can see that Michael." I asked him to take off his sunglasses because it's a pet hate of mine when I'm doing a one-on-one session, but he looked so rough that I asked him to put them back on – a first for me! He was uber cool and lived the rock star dream to the max and died young and still in his prime – he almost followed the immortality script to the letter and his legacy lives on.

Rock & Pop Legends

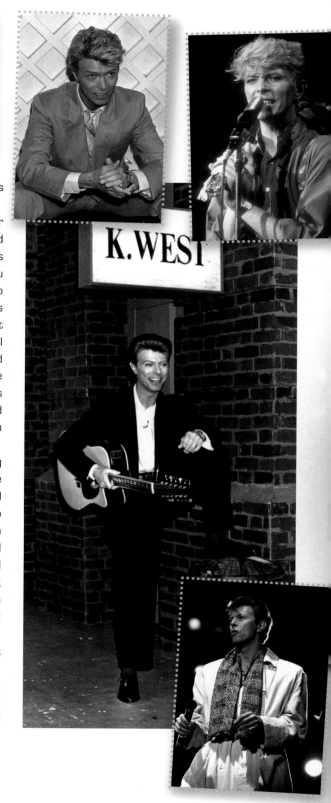

David Bowie

Working with your heroes is never easy and David Bowie slots very nicely into that category. I grew up loving his music so to be able to work closely with him on various occasions in later years has obviously been fantastic. I photographed him on his Glass Spider Tour and at various events and he is never less than fascinating with his various looks, smart clothes and different coloured eyes.

Whether he is holding a Macbeth skull on stage, holding an inflatable leg over his shoulder or performing a duet with the likes of Tina Turner and Freddie Mercury, you always come away with a great image.

On another occasion when I was invited to cover the American leg of his Sound and Vision Tour, it was all arranged in black and white and so it wasn't as visually interesting as some of his other concerts. I shot the whole session with the understanding that Bowie had the final approval on what was put out and what wasn't and so I left everything I'd shot with him and waited for his selections.

We were moving around quite a bit from place to place but I was devastated to find that he'd left them in some hotel room – the whole session! It wasn't as though I wouldn't be photographing him again, but sometimes you have to bite your lip and accept that's the kind of things pop stars sometimes do. I re-shot the concert the following night and all was well in the world again so my not blowing a fuse was totally justified – besides, this was the Thin White Duke I was dealing with.

We all travelled as one to the next gig in another state and there is a code of behaviour that you need to adhere to when in the company of major stars and one of the strictest unwritten rules is that you don't sit next to the artist you are there to photograph – it just doesn't work like that. On this occasion I was sat down when Bowie came and sat next to me and I thought, 'Shit. They'll all think I came and sat next to him.' The reason he'd parked himself beside me, however, was because he wanted to look at my copy of Viz! I took a few pics of him reading Viz and they started running a David Bowie column, which was quite funny and I felt in someway responsible for that.

On another occasion he was headlining Glastonbury and I was told to get along because he was wearing an amazing Alistair McQueen coat and there was an opportunity to shoot a quick studio session before he went on stage. They gave me a Triple-A pass and I got the pictures I needed and was on my way back to London before he'd started his fifth number and that's typical of the kind of quick turnaround jobs I have to do – I say have to! – I'd do it for free when I'm photographing people like David Bowie, Bono and Paul McCartney!

The last set of pictures I took of Bowie were at the Isle of Wight festival where he was headlining. It was while England were playing in the 2006 World Cup and the organisers decided to put the match on the big screens and delayed the start of

Rock & Pop Legends

the concert. For advanced publicity shots, I suggested we get Bowie watching the match on his tour bus, which he agreed to. He wasn't dressed up, had no make-up on and he looked washed out and not particularly well. At one point he just threw a hissy fit at the PR guy and I said to Bowie that if he wasn't happy with any of the pictures, they would never see the light of day – which they haven't. It was totally out of character, however, and despite him performing on stage later that day and looking amazing, just a few days later he had his heart scare and he hasn't done very much since leaving everyone to wonder when he will tour again. Let's hope it's not too long before he's back doing what he does best.

Rock & Pop Legends

ACCESS
ALL
AREAS

Tina Turner

Tina Turner once sang the record 'Simply the Best' and in my eyes, that's exactly what she is. A legend in music, stunning and the consummate professional, I can honestly say that having the opportunity to work with Tina over the past three decades has been an absolute pleasure.

PR guru Bernard Docherty first introduced me to her when he called up and asked whether I wanted to go to Brazil with him to cover Tina's HBO concert in Rio – I believe that's what is known commonly as a no-brainer and I think I'd packed my bags before I'd even finished the phone call. It was an incredible trip and I managed to get some fantastic pictures of Tina immersed in various aspects of Brazilian culture such as samba dancing, football and a selection of other images that were sent around the world. Tina invited me to stay in Rio for a New Year's Eve party and at midnight, thousands of candles were placed in the sand on the beach and flowers were offered to the Gods. Tina had a handful of roses to throw into the sea and was flanked by two secret service guys and I just had to get the picture of her walking towards the ocean with hundreds of candles providing a spectacular backdrop and the only way I could get the angle I needed was to go out several feet in front of her which meant wading out in my tuxedo up to my waste. Tina couldn't stop laughing. "You'd really do anything to get this shot, wouldn't you?" I told her that I wasn't going to miss this once-in-a-

lifetime shot just because of a bit of water and as she walked into the water to throw the roses out, the two secret service guys waded out at the side.

Afterwards, her manager Roger Davies told Bernard Docherty that from then on, whenever I wanted to go out and take pictures of Tina, it was fine and that's how I got my AAA pass with one of the world's greatest female artists.

Since then I've worked with her on the shoot for her James Bond record 'Goldeneye' and at her 50th birthday party at her home, on stage with David Bowie and on several other occasions and the woman is amazing, looks fantastic and is great fun to be around. She is respected by all the people who work with her and the reason she looks so fantastic is that, so long as she isn't on stage, she'll be tucked in bed by 10pm – she looks after herself properly, eats only the best food and drinks the best champagne. I think Tina is coming to England again soon on tour and I'll be there to record her every move – what a lady!

Rock & Pop Legends

Main Picture: Janet Jackson brings audience participation to a new level. **From left top to bottom:** Eurythmics, Ringo Starr and Barbara Bach. **From right top to bottom:** Genesis, A-ha, Sting, Adam Ant, J-Lo and P Diddy and George Michael.

Rock & Pop Legends

Screen Icons

Screen Icons

£3M HOTEL
BILL FOR
LIZ'S NEW
BOYFRIEN

A selection of the stars of the small and silver screen I have photographed over the years, including a great shot of Jonathan Ross and Dame Helen Mirren at the BAFTA's in 2007.

Screen Icons

The Osbournes

The first time I really met Ozzy Osbourne was through Gary Bushell who was then a columnist on The Sun. We'd been invited out to his house in Los Angeles and though we'd crossed paths a number of times over the years, we'd never met socially, so to speak. When we arrived at his home, I was surprised to find Ozzy had shaved all his hair off and looked more like an accountant than the Prince of Darkness and Sharon's weight had ballooned. Their home wasn't as I expected either, and was full of white shag pile carpets and white leather sofas and I was asking myself, 'Where's the goth in this?' Then, shortly after arriving, Ozzy said, "I've got to go and pick my kids up from school." Sharon went out and Gary went with Ozzy to do the interview on the way to school, leaving me to look after Jack and Kelly. I didn't mind and was on all fours letting them clamber over me but it was a bit surreal to say the least.

We did some great family shots when everyone returned and Ozzy was trying to cover up the little ones whose nappies had fallen off. At that point, Ozzy's only real claim to fame tabloid-wise was biting the head off a bat, so it was unusual to do a story like that but it showed him in a completely different light to the one he was perhaps perceived in previously.

The next time I saw him was at the MTV awards in New York and Ozzy was like a little schoolboy. He came up to me and said, "Sharon's given me $500 – come and play!" I had a job to do and no assistant to help me out, so reluctantly I had to decline the offer – something I've always regretted.

A few years later, Ozzy was massive across the

The Osbournes

"Ozzy had shaved all his hair off and looked more like an accountant than the Prince of Darkness."

world and headlining the Rock in Rio festival on Copa Cabana beach. It was winter in England but glorious sunshine in Rio and that trip was memorable for a number of reasons. I met Ozzy in a hotel foyer and he wanted to meet The Great Train Robber, Ronnie Biggs, who of course was living in Rio at the time. Biggs was like royalty back then and all the rock stars wanted to meet him and have their photograph taken with him because he was the one man who'd said "F**k you!" to the establishment – and got away with it. He held barbecues at his home for guests from Britain and for $350 he'd get a suckling pig, beers and you'd have the most amazing time. Ronnie would occasionally write to me and ask me to bring T-bags, HP sauce, marmalade and other items unique to Britain whenever I went to Brazil.

I went out and got rat-faced every night while I was there and because there was no deadline for the pictures, I kept them all on one film and had the camera with me when I went out on a bender. I got into a taxi and just about managed to tell him where I needed to go and when he pulled up at the hotel, the camera slid under my seat and I forgot all about it. The next day, I woke up with a sore head – and no camera. I tried to think what I'd done the previous evening and then worked out I must have left it in the taxi, so I called Ronnie Biggs up and told him what had happened. He told me to leave it to him and he must have then put the word out on the street that he wanted the camera returning ASAP. By the end of the day, he'd tracked it down, but told

The Osbournes

"I forgot we had this f * * * * *g house."

me the finder wanted a reward. I was given a time and place to meet him and went along, believing he wanted $100 as a reward. When I arrived, he told me he now wanted $200 – in all honesty, I didn't really care what he wanted as long as I got the pictures back. If only the picture desk knew what I'd gone through to get them!

I did a couple of other awards ceremonies with Ozzy before the MTV show 'The Osbournes' first aired, and put Ozzy and his family into a completely different league. Suddenly all the pics I'd done of the Osbournes from up to 15 years earlier were in big demand and when he was next over to the UK, I was invited to their mansion in Buckinghamshire for a photo shoot. Ozzy was looking great with his hands covered in rings and as we moved from room to room he turned to me and said, "I forgot we had this f * * * * *g house."

Ozzy and Sharon are good people and I know that because of the people they keep around them. Ozzy's assistant, Tony, has been with him for 20 or more years and people who are b * * * * * * s don't keep staff for that long because they don't put up with them. Sharon and Ozzy once organised a Tears in Heaven cover version featuring dozens of great names from rock to raise funds for the Tsunami disaster and she paid for me to go over to the States and cover the event by cashing in her air miles – Sharon, who looks a million dollars has completely transformed herself over the years and is the power and the brains behind the organisation, make no mistake and she's a great woman. When

Gary Farrow asked me to do a few frames to promote the cover of her autobiography, we went into her kitchen where a chef was preparing food and I asked her when was the last time she'd actually cooked in there and she told me she didn't think she'd ever cooked in there! So we got a picture of her holding a frying pan with her dog in it and another one with Ozzy biting the dog.

I've shot pictures for various videos and other events such as The Prince's Trust and Ozzy and Sharon remain two of my favourite people and their friendly, dysfunctional family is a loveable version of The Addams Family for modern times.

The Osbournes

Girls Aloud

Girls Aloud

Girls Aloud were plucked from obscurity after winning Popstars: The Rivals and are some of the most beautiful girls in pop today.

ACCESS **ALL** AREAS

Girls Aloud

Kylie

Stock, Aitken and Waterman discovered a host of home-grown stars in the early eighties before turning their attention to the Aussie soap stars and Kylie Minogue was one of the first to arrive on these shores. She turned up in London looking cute and gorgeous, but with awful permed hair and clothes - and so began a nation's love affair with the future princess of pop.

I shot her many times and, of course, for a while the main focus was on whether she was seeing Jason Donovan or not. They denied it and the 'is she, isn't she?' stories were front page news for quite a while. I shot Kylie and Jason at the Royal Variety Show as they sang together, looking lovingly into each other's eyes, but still denying they were an item – though everyone knew they were at it! The mystery and pretence kept the interest alive so their denial was understandable.

There was a Stock, Aitken and Waterman version of 'Do They Know It's Christmas?' in 1987 and I took a terrific picture of Bros and Jason Donovan lifting Kylie, who was wearing hot-pants, though not those golden hot pants that later almost brought a nation of British men to their knees!

I travelled to Australia to cover Jason filming a film called 'Heroes' and Kylie was in 'The Delinquents'. They were the commodities of the day and their legion of fans couldn't get enough of them. In fact, The Sun's legendary editor, Kelvin McKenzie, reckoned 'Neighbours' was the biggest thing since sliced bread and so sent me Down Under for three months to do a 'Neighbours' special. We were doing

Kylie

"I shot her many times and, of course, for a while the main focus was on whether she was seeing Jason Donovan or not."

stickers albums of the show and it was huge business for the paper and they gave me a big bag of cash to buy every picture of Kylie, Jason and other cast members available. I spent three months in a hotel suite gathering pictures, paying photographers and buying their rights to each picture. Everything was happening in Australia at that time and I actually

Kylie

ACCESS
ALL
AREAS

thought I might end up living there at one point because there was no competition – it was wide open and reporter Neil Wallace and I were mopping up. I think we had about 26 centre spreads on Kylie and other Neighbours cast members during that three-month period. Incredible.

Then, Miss Goody Two Shoes goes off with one of the biggest Casanova's in the music business – rock god Michael Hutchence. Suddenly I got a call to go and get some pictures of Kylie and Hutchence heading off on the Orient Express for a dirty weekend. They looked totally loved up and became the hottest rock couple on the planet and it added a new, edgier side to Kylie that she hadn't had before and her career path seemed to completely change track. Her clothes changed, her hair changed and her music became very hip – unthinkable a few years earlier.

Then, of course, a couple of years back Kylie announced she had breast cancer, leaving her fans and the pop industry in a state of shock while she went away for treatment and a recovery period. Obviously nobody knew how things would pan out and whether she'd ever be back performing again, but don't let her slight frame fool you – she's a very determined young lady and when it was announced she was making her comeback in Sydney a year or so later, I rang her management and asked if I could fly in and cover her first three numbers and they were more than happy to accommodate me. I was the only English guy to make that journey and I was treated fantastically well and after a few session

Kylie

"It's good to have her back."

pictures promoting her perfume, I covered the eagerly-awaited comeback concert and she came out with feather boas and looked absolutely fantastic. The crowd erupted and I just thought, 'Yeah, good on you.' She's one of the greatest entertainer's of our era and she delivers every time. It's good to have her back.

Kylie

Rod Stewart

Rod and his women – there's a book in that itself! Rod's a terrific guy, football mad but just one of the lads. I went over to L.A one time when he was promoting a new album and had a meal with him after a photo-shoot. As I went for the butter, he grabbed my arm and said, "Hey – watch your cholesterol." When Rod advises you, you tend to listen, especially when you're as health-conscious and healthy-looking as he is. Rod's had several beautiful wives and girlfriends over the years and has enjoyed his fame and wealth to the full and I've been fortunate to work with him many times over the past 25 years.

I recall that the first time I met Penny Lancaster, who Rod married in 2007, was at a soccer six tournament. She came and stood next to me with a camera and she asked who I was and who I worked for. I told her and then asked what she was doing there. "Oh, just photographing my boyfriend." I put two and two together and said, "You're not Rod's girlfriend are you?" She smiled and said, "Er, maybe…" She knew what she was doing and a few moments later went over to him and gave him a hug and kiss, thus introducing herself to the world.

There was another time I went with Dominic Mohan on a boat owned by Sir Philip Green (owner of BHS) with Rod and Penny and I always enjoy his company. I've taken pictures of him playing football over the years and he's even got a football pitch at the back of his house. On one occasion I spotted a model railway enthusiast magazine on a table and I smiled and Rod said, "You're not going to

Rod Stewart

"You're not going to see that Dave."

see that, Dave." Of course, he has a huge model railway, somewhere in his house but that's not for public consumption, apparently!

Rod enjoys his money more than any other star I can think of, he has a beautiful family and has great health and he is, let's not forget, a fantastic singer and entertainer.

Rod Stewart

Mariah Carey

Whenever Mariah Carey hits town, you know you are in the presence of a genuine diva. She has her very own lighting guy and will only be pictured from certain angles. I was once called up by Sony to cover a concert she was performing at the Royal Albert Hall. I was asked to come over for a meeting, where they tried to schedule in another eight meetings to continue discussions! I told them I wasn't going to do that and they were saying that they needed to go over this, that and the other and I said, "Look, I know where and where not to stand. I've done this kind of thing before, you know." They were insistent, telling me they'd pay me to go to the next meeting, then pay me some more to come to another and so on – the money was getting ridiculous. They wanted me to set up a team of people who could help me rush the pictures of the concert to be processed, then return them so Mariah could choose the ones she wanted and then I'd supply various images to a dozen newspapers and magazines around the world.

I told them it was going to be expensive and they told me money was no object and it all went ahead and seemed to go fairly well. I kept a photographic lab open, had a dispatch rider waiting and eventually presented Mariah and her people with a set of proof prints to select from. One of the pictures she was particularly interested in was of a duet she'd done with Luther Vandross. Mariah wanted pictures only taken from the left but they were so far apart, it seemed a bit pointless. At the end of the duet, Mariah walked to the front of the stage with Luther

Mariah Carey

"I told them it was going to be expensive and they told me money was no object."

and she was clutching a big bouquet of flowers and smiling beautifully. It was a great shot, just what I'd been looking for, but when she thumbed through the pictures later, it was "No, no, no, no…" I asked what was wrong and she was saying things like she didn't like the look of her elbow in one image and could I change it? I said there wasn't time to re-touch the picture if they wanted to wire these out immediately and eventually some flunky in her entourage finally said, "That's the one. We're going to use this one." So the picture was sent out and it was so bad I didn't even want my name associated with it but because I'd been paid so much, they said, "Just do it!"

I took it to Associated Press and explained, bad as it was, that was what they wanted and, because money talks, they got their way. Luther Vandross, on the other hand, didn't care so I put out some nice big pictures of Luther and almost all the reviewers used that instead along with a tiny image of Mariah turning the other way! Mariah's people called me up and asked why we hadn't used the one they'd selected and I explained that I knew my job and it was their own fault because the person who chose the picture didn't have a clue. In future, I told them to trust my judgement and if they hired me again, let me do my job and everyone would be happy.

The next day, they asked if I could issue the picture I'd originally wanted to use and send it out instead. I asked them if they knew a phrase containing 'horse, stable, door and bolted'. I told them nobody would re-write their reviews and print the picture that should have been used anyway, a

Mariah Carey

day after the event. The people at Sony were apologetic and tried to explain that they had to do what they were told because Mariah was married to the Head of Sony and I had genuine sympathy for them – and I should have learned from that experience but when they called me again to do a job for them, I accepted it!

I went along to the hotel she was staying at and began setting up my studio and the lighting. I'd no sooner switched the lights on than Mariah's lighting guy came along and popped out all the overhead bulb lights because she didn't like them! They began trying to dictate the lighting I should use and they insisted I use theirs and the end result was exactly as I'd feared. They put so many conditions about what I could take pictures of and what I couldn't, plus certain angles I had to do that I ended up with completely unflattering pictures that were half as good as they could have been and made her look completely bonkers in all honesty.

I was asked to present an award to Mariah for best single or something on one occasion because nobody from Bizarre could make it. On the award itself, there was a picture of Mariah. Her PA said, "Oh no. You can't give her that. She won't like that picture at all. It's not very flattering." I asked what he wanted me to do and he said, "Do you have your camera with you?" I told him I had and he told me to set-up a studio and take a new picture that could be superimposed on top of the other. I said it seemed like a lot of fuss over nothing, but he insisted I should do it – so I did. I went and got my

Mariah Carey

"She is a modern-day Liz Taylor!."

gear, set up the studio and shot a new picture to replace the inch-sized image of Mariah holding the award that was already on the award! Confused? I was! I thought Mariah and the people around her must be barking mad, but that's what can happen when you've got too much money and Mariah Carey remains my ultimate diva for very obvious reasons – she is a modern-day Liz Taylor!

Mariah Carey

Duran Duran

John Taylor, Roger Taylor, Andy Taylor, Nick Rhodes and Simon Le Bon – when Duran Duran first started out, they were the ultimate pin-up band. If you shot them at that time, you'd be guaranteed to earn up to £30,000 from the picture which could be sold again and again around the world – they were that big.

I was given incredible access to the lads in those early years and went out on tour with them and did as much stuff as I wanted – but it was never going to last. The bigger they got, the more buffers appeared in-between them and people like myself, but it was too late – the editor had been given this unlimited access and was hungry for the next big story, so in effect, they'd created their own monster and the end result was me, almost shot in the head by the Duran boys – let me explain...

They'd gone over to the South of France to record a new album and I was sent over to get some pictures to accompany a story of some sort. I started out by going around the youth bars in Nice asking the local kids if they'd heard of Duran Duran, only to be told, "Non," time after time. Eventually, one guy said he had heard of them and thought they were staying in a villa up in the hills. After getting rough directions, I set off to find my quarry and after a while, echoing across the fields, I could hear the unmistakable sound of 'Rio' reverberating towards me. It was coming from a huge chateau that looked impregnable and I wondered how the hell I was supposed to snatch pictures of the band, who were somewhere deep within this magnificent fortress. This, however, is where the SAS tactics

Duran Duran

ACCESS **ALL** AREAS

and adrenaline instincts kick in and because legendary Sun editor Kelvin McKenzie had placed his trust in me and had given me such a fantastic opportunity to make a career for myself as a celebrity photographer, I was desperate to repay his faith and I was going to go that extra mile for him, even if it killed me. I had to make it work, so I scrambled through the undergrowth at the back of the chateau and managed to get to a position near to the back door, while being reasonably camouflaged.

I was confident that, at some point, they would come out for a break and sure enough, the music eventually stopped and the door opened. Out walks Simon Le Bon with his girlfriend at the time, Claire Stansfield and he started groping her over the back of a car. I was thinking, 'Shit! This is one step down from being a peeping Tom!' Regardless, it was click, there's a picture, click, there's another picture – and so on. I was, however, about to almost pay the ultimate price for my covert operation as Roger and Nick Taylor then came out with an air rifle and started shooting pellets into the undergrowth, fooling around. The problem was, they didn't know I was there and the pellets were missing me by inches! As it happened, I survived intact and processed the pics successfully.

A lot of our tip offs came from their own PR people who would tell us who was appearing where and at what time because it would be good for their client to appear in The Sun, particularly if they were trying to promote something.

I bought a bright red Porsche 911 Targa and there was another memorable incident with Duran Duran that kind of illustrates how things used to be. They were appearing on The Wogan Show so I went along and as promised; they came out and posed for a few pictures after rehearsals. Afterwards, it became a game of cat and mouse. The boys were in a Mercedes limo with me in hot pursuit and at one point both cars were doing in excess of 100mph along London's Westway. As I pulled alongside the limo, John Taylor began to moon at me from the passenger window. I was trying to grab my camera while staying in control of the car, but I just missed my chance. Then they pulled into Regents Park and I parked behind. I walked over towards them but they ran out on the blindside, got in my Porsche and drove off! I was stood in the middle of the road taking a few pictures and then they pulled up about 200 yards away. Nick Rhodes shouted, "Dave! Here's your keys!" and dropped them by the kerb. They then left my car with its doors open before their limo pulled alongside and drove them away. It was a game, no more, and one we all willingly took part in and the message was pretty clear – it was a case of 'we'll work with you on our terms but when we've had enough we'll tell you to f***k off.' Fair enough!

I've continued to get pictures of the band over the years and they showed they still had what it takes to be rock stars at the Diana Concert a few years back. They've been away, come back, gone away and come back again and I've been there with them through it all and enjoyed every minute of it.

Duran Duran

The Brits

The Brits

From left to right: Wet Wet Wet, Zoe Ball and Norman Cook, Westlife, Caprice, Annie Lennox, Rod Stewart and Rachel Hunter. **Main Picture:** Sam Fox and Mick Fleetwood, the most unlikely presenting partnership in history.

Main Picture: Eminem on one of his rare UK appearances. **From top to bottom:** Elton presenting Eminem with his Best International Male Brit Award, Noel Gallagher on stage with U2, Bono performing with U2, Chris Martin of Coldplay and finally Pink.

The Brits

ACCESS **ALL** AREAS

The Brits

Main Picture: A stunning Beyonce Knowles. **From left to right:** Justin Hawkins of The Darkness, 50 Cent, Bryan McFadden and Kerry Katona, an early picture of Amy Winehouse – pre tattoos and Scarlett Johansson.

Main Picture: A jaw dropping Scissor Sisters set. **From left to right:** Chris Evans, Billie Piper and Gazza, Chris Evans and Gazza, Gwen Stefani and Girls Aloud.

The Brits

The Brits

Main Picture: Mark Ronson and a painfully thin Amy Winehouse. **From top to bottom:** Ricky Wilson of The Kaiser Chiefs and Chris Martin of Coldplay.

From top to bottom: Amy Winehouse, Lily Allen, The Arctic Monkeys, Rihanna and The Osbournes.

The Brits

Natasha Bedingfield

Natasha Bedingfield

The underwater shot of Natasha is one of the most striking photographs I have ever taken. She is now a huge star in the States and is great fun to work with.

"Hanging out on a shoot with Dave in one of the most beautiful spots I've been to in the world, Bermuda, was an experience I will remember and cherish forever. It seems so funny to think that we were actually working that day! We were having far too much fun to think of it as work. Dave is a genuinely lovely and real man, something that is rare in this business... He is also one of the best photographers out there. I hope that we have many more times together like this..." **Natasha Bedingfield**

Natasha Bedingfield

Gorgeous Girls

Gorgeous Girls

Main Picture left: Louise Redknapp. **Main Picture right:** Pink. **From left to right:** Keeley Hazell, Scarlett Johansson, Myleene Klass, Beyonce, Halle Berry, Kate Beckinsale, Rachel Stevens, Eva Longoria Parker, Patsy Kensit, Charlize Theron, Fearne Cotton and Holly Willoughby, Kelly Brook and Angelina Jolie.

Gorgeous Girls

Little Britain

What can I say about these guys? Matt Lucas and David Walliams – always a pleasure to take pictures of and I have some fantastic images of the guys on tour with various guests such as Kate Moss, Chris Moyles and Paul McCartney and I hope they will keep doing what they do for many years.

David wrote to me once, thanking me for a set of pictures I took – he's a massive star now, but it hasn't changed him at all – how many stars of his calibre would do that? It's my favourite TV show so I was delighted when I was asked to shoot a Comic Relief show at Hampstead Odeon that was made into a Christmas DVD with all proceeds going to the charity – it was two of the funniest hours I've spent in my life. Every guest they got up on stage was totally humiliated, as expected and the pictures speak for themselves and are guaranteed to raise a smile…

Little Britain

"David wrote to me once,
thanking me for a set
of pictures I took."

ACCESS
ALL
AREAS

Little Britain

Coldplay

Chris Martin had a huge boil on his neck for the first set of Coldplay pictures I took. They were just starting off and they were really grateful for the coverage they got because not long after, they became huge, but they all seem down-to-earth lads who have remembered their roots.

I met Chris properly at the recording of Band Aid 2 in 2004. I was setting up a studio to take stills of everybody taking part and Chris arrived about 8am before there was even any press waiting outside. He asked if I needed a hand – he had to be somewhere by 10am so he sat there with me just chatting for a while. He said, "I'm really pissed off." I asked him why. He said, "I've never really wanted to be photographed with Gwyneth because we're not interested in that showbiz-type angle but the other day we were out on Primrose Hill and this French guy came up to us. He was with his young daughter and asked if he could take a picture because his little girl was a huge fan of the band. So I sat on a bench overlooking London and his daughter sat next to me. Then he asked if he could take a picture of Gwyneth with his daughter, only he got Gwyneth to sit on the other side of the bench. That was it and I thought no more about it until I was flicking through a French magazine and there's a picture of me next to Gwyneth on that same bench. The bastard had cut out his daughter and re-touched the picture to make it look like we were sat together!"

I've done some devious things, but I'd never stoop that low!

Chris is a terrific, grounded lad and you'd never guess he fronted one of the biggest bands in the world. His outlook on life and being famous might not be good for people in my profession, but it's very refreshing, all the same.

Coldplay

ACCESS **ALL** AREAS

Coldplay

Upcoming Talent

Upcoming Talent

Main Picture: The Feeling. **From left to right:** Leona Lewis, The Kooks, Lily Allen and Keith, Mark Ronson, The Editors, Rihanna, Amy Winehouse, Razorlight, Duffy, Adele and Natasha Bedingfield.

ACCESS **ALL** AREAS

Upcoming Talent

153

Gordon Brown

In 2007 my wife Janice and I bought a large Georgian manor house near to the picturesque seaside town of Southwold in Suffolk, with a view to renting it out for everything from private stays, through to film shoots and weddings. My first customer was the film-maker Richard Curtis, famous for the box office hits Four Weddings and a Funeral and Love Actually, who said he had a 'famous client' interested in booking the house for two weeks in August 2008. Knowing Richard had another movie on the boil and his penchant for employing Hollywood megastars for cameo roles, I spent many idle moments daydreaming about Angelina Jolie or Julia Roberts sweeping down my driveway.

After years of being eyeballed and strong-armed by various minders, I know security is an issue with celebrities, but even I was taken aback when two FBI-style security guys turned up to check the house out, asking questions such as how secure the perimeter was and was I aware of any weak spots?

In the meantime, a quad bike was stolen from our garden and, making the usual call to police purely for insurance purposes, fully expected the same lacklustre response you expect over what, these days, is regarded as a minor incident.

So when two detectives arrived at the house, taking an avid interest in every fine detail of the theft, we were genuinely surprised. When they installed a tracking system in our outhouse, saying it was to monitor any further intrusion on our property, the surprise turned to bemused astonishment.

It wasn't until two weeks later, when six Special Branch officers turned up to erect tank traps and temporary traffic lights on our driveway that the penny finally dropped. Our special treatment had nothing to do with Suffolk police being especially welcoming to new homeowners, and everything to do with the mystery guest we were expecting the following week.

"Don't you know who it is yet?" asked a Special Branch officer as I watched them casing every inch of the joint, feeling like the village idiot.

Taking pity on me, he said that as it was probably going to leak out anyway, he'd better let me know that whilst David Cameron was holidaying in Cornwall, my house would be playing host to the Prime Minister Gordon Brown and his family.

There I was, someone who has made a career out of knowing the whereabouts of every famous person this side of Osama Bin Laden, with not the faintest clue that my own house was about to be the centre of a big story in the next day's newspapers.

"But he can't be!" I exclaimed. "Does he know what I do? I'm a Sun photographer for Christ's sake!"

He assured me that the PM had been fully briefed and, from that point on, my life became a whirlwind of top secret information and covert operations, my own mind racing with thoughts such as "will my Direct Line insurance cover a terrorist attack?" They assured me that should an Exocet missile hit my roof, the government would foot the repair bill.

But most weirdly of all, I suddenly found the press lurking outside my house, trying to get photos of the grounds and glean small snippets of information about the layout and furnishings. I simply referred them to the Downing Street press office, as I had been instructed to do. I was in a TV shop and balked as I saw overhead shots of my house beamed across all 20 screens, then later that day a friend called to say there was live footage running of me sitting on my terrace.

At first, it was all very amusing, but my humour started to curdle slightly when various Downing Street minions came crawling out of the woodwork, making last-minute demands such as putting up 'bomb-proof' curtains (not sure my local Tesco sells those), and moving the washing machine in to the main house because the Browns wanted to be self-sufficient and have everything under one roof. Fair enough.

But when, the day before the PM arrived, a rather abrupt woman rang to say that a couple of my framed photographs hung around the property were deemed 'inappropriate' (the alleged main culprit being a picture of Michael Jackson dancing on stage) I blew my top and said, in so many words, that if they didn't like it, they could find somewhere else to stay.

I had tolerated my house being turned in to a military zone, allowed endless detectives to trudge around the place, put up curtains and even re-plumbed for them, but being asked to remove the pictures I'm immensely proud of was a step too far.

Gordon Brown

..AND GORDON STARTS HIS HOLIDAY AT PAPARAZZI TOWERS

[newspaper article text, largely illegible]

BIG SHOT: Photographer Dave Hogan is the Browns' holiday host

PREMIER HOME: Shadingfield Hall is Georgian

SMILES BETTER: Gordon and Sarah at Whitlingham park, Norfolk, yesterday

PM set for a warm reception

PROTEST: Coastal plea coincides with holid...

By Mark Lord

PRIME Minister Gordon Brown has been promised a "very warm" welcome in the Southwold area this weekend – and it will just be because of the promised hot weather.

[remaining article text illegible]

For the record, I don't think for one minute that any of these demands originated from the Prime Minister or his wife, but from the lower ranks of Downing Street officialdom trying to justify their existence.

The Browns proved to be perfect, trouble-free houseguests, who left lovely thank you notes for us and our children, thanking them for the use of their toys. Now I know what to expect, I hope they come back next year.

Funny really. It was the ultimate Access All Areas happening in my own home, but I wasn't invited.

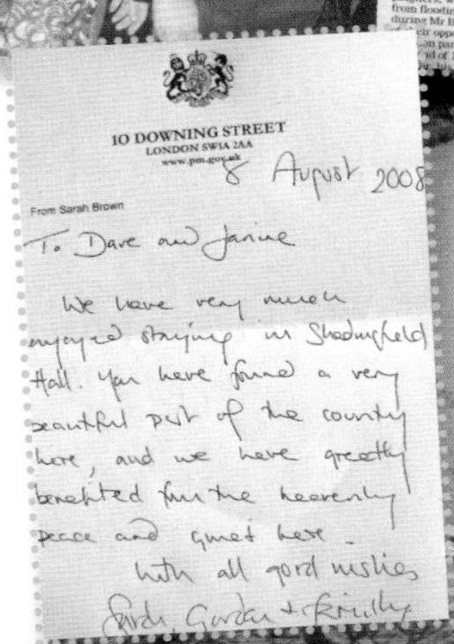

10 DOWNING STREET
LONDON SW1A 2AA
www.pm.gov.uk

From Sarah Brown

8 August 2008

To Dave and Janne

We have very much enjoyed staying in Shadingfield Hall. You have found a very beautiful part of the country here, and we have greatly benefited from the heavenly peace and quiet here.

With all good wishes

Sarah Gordon + Family

Gordon Brown

The Editors
& Favourite Images

John Blake was the first Bizarre editor I worked with and it was at a time when nobody was really covering the pop industry in any depth. He was being offered trips around the world on an almost daily basis and eventually, I flew out with him to cover Men At Work in Sydney. We went to Barbados covering Eddy Grant another week and it was a case of who shall we cover next and in which country? We could have gone anywhere we wanted and never been out of the air – it was wide open at the time and John Blake was the first real showbiz columnist of that era to take full advantage.

Probably the most successful editor I ever worked with, and one who now has a top-rated TV show on either side of the Atlantic, is Piers Morgan. We go back a long way and we became very good friends over the years and I'm not surprised at all that he's gone on to be a such a major star. He's always had the ability to take the piss out of himself and he told me about his experiences in America and how they don't quite get his humour. In the States, it's all about who has the biggest trailer so on America's Got Talent, he told the producers, "I demand a smaller trailer than David Hasselhoff! I can't have him having a smaller trailer than me!" Of course, it's all a piss-take, but if you don't know Piers, you probably wouldn't be able to tell whether he's being serious or not. I spent five years of my life travelling the world with him and he's a guy that made the most out of every opportunity passed his way – he was brilliant at it.

We once went along to the Cannes Film Festival

The Editors

and had absolutely nothing set up. The Mail on Sunday would have contracted interviews with Michael Douglas and Sharon Stone whereas Piers would simply approach Sharon and say, "Hello – pleased to meet you. I'm Piers Morgan from The Sun. I loved your film." I'd take a picture of them both chatting and he'd go on from there, get his questions in, maybe adapt a few translated paragraphs from a French magazine interview to beef it up and hey presto, we'd have a great centre spread. Piers went on to edit The News of the World and later The Mirror before moving into television. He'll probably go on to be the next Parkinson, because he's never afraid to ask near the knuckle questions, but he can do it in such a way that he'll be able to get away with it, too.

Andy Coulson was the best schmoozer I ever worked with. He'd get stars calling him up saying that they'd been caught with their trousers down and he'd always tell them to come in, be honest and we'd do the story. He told them they'd get a kicking, but so long as they told the truth – and told him everything – he'd be able to control the story and it would be a case of damage limitation. He was a diplomat par excellence and after going on to edit The News of the World, he is now the driving force behind David Cameron's press campaign and if anyone can help Cameron into No.10, it will be Andy.

Kelvin McKenzie gave me my first job and for that, I'm forever in his debt. He is a legendary Sun editor who was fiercely protective of his staff and didn't take shit from anybody. If I ever had problems

of any kind – including the odd death threat or kneecapping from managers who didn't like the fact I'd revealed their client had a girlfriend or whatever in a snatched photo – he'd be on the phone to them immediately with legal threats and the threat of a lifetime ban from The Sun – which could effectively end an artist's career – believe me, when Kelvin counter-threatened, they listened.

Dominic Mohan is totally into the music scene and he was one of the few tabloid journalists to earn respect from bands like Oasis because he knows his stuff and they knew he knew. Dominic is the next editor-in-waiting from the Murdoch stable.

Victoria Newton was The Sun's LA correspondent who built up the most amazing contacts in America and that's led to her being one of the chief feature writers at The Sun with a glittering future ahead of her.

Currently, the Bizarre editor is Gordon Smart who is young, sharp and incredibly close to the likes of Noel Gallagher, Kasabian and all the top young new bands. He's got a more laddish approach to the column and is doing his own thing, which clearly seems to be working. They are all bright, incredibly talented people – past and present – who deliver the goods, time after time and make whatever I do 10 times better. They've been a pleasure to work with so far and if you get the right combination of writer and photographer, you're unstoppable. Today, I can walk into any room and take pictures of royalty, rock stars or movie stars and take control for 30 seconds without causing embarrassment or offence

The Editors

"Hogie is the greatest showbiz photographer in newspapers. He's witnessed and put up with more tantrums and celebrity nonsense than any other snapper and yet is still as enthusiastic today as he was on day one. In the 18 years I've known him he's never failed to get the picture and this book only scratches the surface of his amazing career."

Andy Coulson

and get an image that can be used in the paper the next day. That's what people I take pictures of want – somebody who can be decisive, take pictures and then f** k off out of the way. They know I'm not their best friend, I'm there to do a job and as long as everyone understands that, I'll hopefully continue to get Access All Areas for many years to come.

The Editors

Here is just a small selection of my personal favourite photographs, from the Brixton riots to The Incredibles, my wife Janice and children Josh, Harry & Liv. I have lived the lifestyle and seen people and places that most of us can only dream of, I wouldn't change a thing!

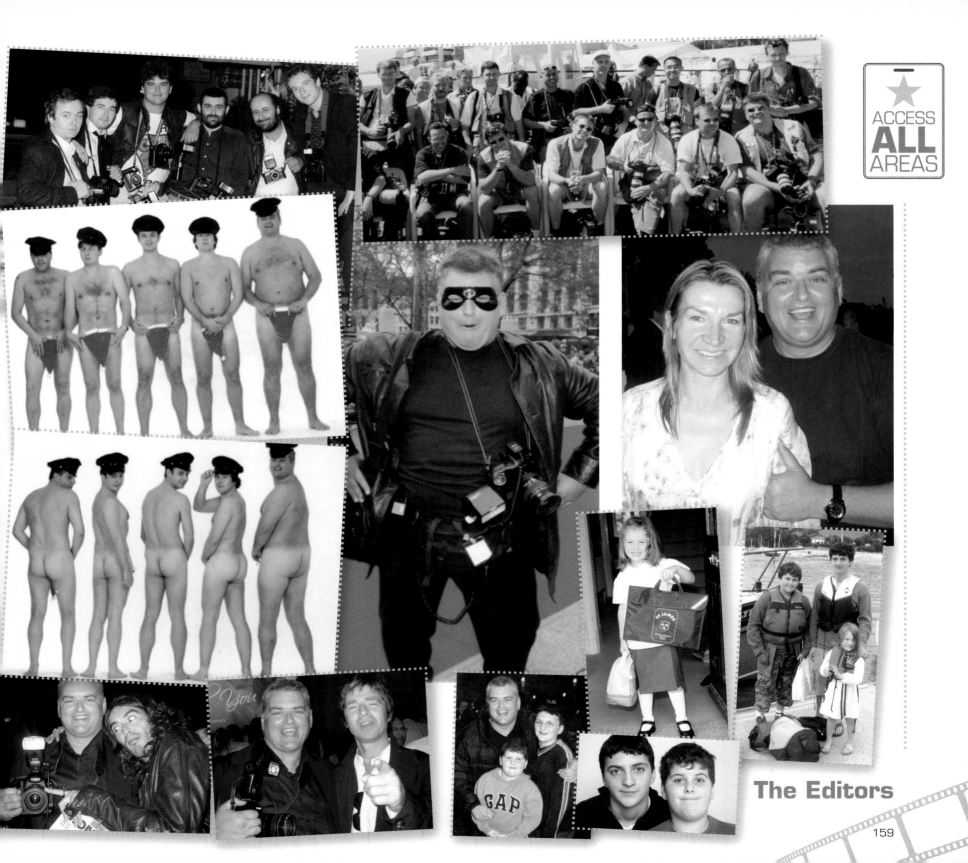

The Editors

Acknowledgements

I'd like to thank my wife Janice, and my kids Josh, Harry and Olivia for putting up with my chaotic lifestyle and giving me the space to do my job.

My Dad. My brother Philip for his steadfast support and common sense. Thank god someone in the family has some!

My close friends: David and Lucy, Libby, Marian, Ellie, Stella, Pat, Sue, Jon and Jo.

I wouldn't be anywhere without the great team of support behind me. Heartfelt thanks go to my long suffering assistant, Claire Greenway. As we go to print she's just about to have her baby. I simply don't know how I'm going to cope without her for the next couple of months. Hurry back Claire!

My P.A. Caron Westbrook, who puts up with all my disorganisation, missing receipts and last minute rearrangements with her unflagging good humour and cheerfulness.

Special thanks to my colleagues at the Sun – editor Rebekah Wade, Dominic Mohan, Victoria Newton, John Edwards and all the great people I've worked with down the years on the Sun Picture desk. A big thank you to Gordon Smart who I've had the pleasure to work with over the last year, Emma Smith and everyone who's worked on the Bizarre team, which has been my home since 1980.

I've been lucky to have worked with some brilliant editors, Kelvin Mackenzie, John Blake, Piers Morgan, Andy Coulson, among others. A fantastic bunch of guys to work with. Thanks for all the breaks, laughs and friendship down the years.

My colleagues at Getty Images – Nick Evans-Lombe, Adrian Murrell, George DeKeerle, Jennifer Stanley, Julia Galleway, Andy Smith, Steve Munday, Steve Blogg. And a big thank you to Rick Mayston for setting up the book and believing there was a book in me!

Those work colleagues who support me night in, night out – Dave Benett, Richard Young, Alan Davidson, Ian West, James Peltekian, Gareth Cattermole, Gareth Davies, Jane Moore, Jon Furniss, Dave Fisher, Mike Marsden, Sue Moore and Frank Micelotta and my new assistant Fergus McDonald.

My publishing team at Green Umbrella, Kevin and Vanessa Gardner who have done such a fantastic job on the book and writer David Clayton who has put together my memories so well.

My support team at home – our super-organised nanny Lubica Pandza, Shadingfield Hall uber-efficient housekeeper Julie Rye and her wonderful daughters Emma and Rachel

Jonathan Morrish, who is the most trusted person in the UK and set up the Jackson Access.

Helen Oldfield at Astute PR, Mark Borkoski PR, Genaro at HMV, Radio 1 press office, Virgin press office, David Koppel of St. Giles Gallery, Aimee Lake and Lucie Speciale at Sony.

And to all those PRs, impressarios and backers that have greased my path down the years –

Alan Edwards and the Outside Organisation
Moira and Barbara at MBC Publicity
Gary Farrow
DDA
Sony BMG
RCA Press Office
Murray Chalmers
Stuart Bell at MPL
MOBO
Mercury Music Awards
Wembley
The Vue
Grosvenor House
NEC
Andy Holmes at HSBC Private Bank

Bernard and Maria at LD Publicity
Nik and Toby at Freud Communications
Premier PR
Pete Reynolds at BAFTA
Kate Head
RDW Management
Jonathan Shalit
The Brits
NME Awards
World Music Awards
The Odeon West End
Empire Cinema
Koko
Fenton Higgins

PRESS

Dave Hogan

The Sun

TV Quick Awards

KING ARTHUR

PHOTOGRAPHER - FOYER

DIE HARD 4.0

PHOTOGRAPHER

SMASH HITS
POLL WINNERS PARTY
1997
IN ASSOCIATION WITH
our price

MEDIA
Photographer

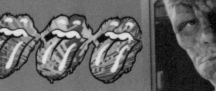
GILLETTE

RADIO

MEDIA

Andy Coulson
Freud Communications Event

CHARLOTTE GRAY

TOAST

FANTASTIC 4
UK PREMIERE

VH1
MUSIC FIRST

97 fashion awards

The Theatre at
Madison Square Garden
October 24, 1997

2559

ONE ON ONE

6 MTV

NON-TRANSFERABLE

FOREIGN AFFAIR

Herbie
fully loaded

Photographer

DAILY BUG

PHOTO

PHOTOGRAPHER

BRIT

GRAND
AFTER

GUEST

EXECUTIVE CLUB
BRITISH AIRWAYS

DAVE HOGAN

76693548

presents

MALIBU
MOBO
MOBO III
THE AWARDS

BRIT AWARDS 98

Sponsored by
Britannia Music Club B

london
9/2/98

194

THE OLYM
TORCH CONC

LONDON · JUNE

ROY
ALBERT
WEDNE
15th OC
200

LOUNGE
ACCESS

WORLD PREMIERE

GUEST HOUSE
PARADISO

WEDNESDAY 24TH NOVEMBER 1999

PRESS PASS - CINEMA ONLY

PHOTOCALL		
OUVERTURE	**14**	
THE SUN		
		56
PHOTOGRAPHE		

101
DALMATIANS
MUSIC IS REAL

ERT HALL
R 1996

54ᵉ FESTIVAL INTERNATIONAL
DU FILM - CANNES 9-20 MAI

David John
HOGAN

2001

THE SUN
ROYAUME-UNI

THE MAN WHO CRIED 12

PRESS

SUMMER
ROBBIE
WILLIAMS
LIVE AT
KNEBWORTH

THE
WORLD
PREMIERE

Proudly Presented by smart

PRESS

AROUND THE WORLD
IN 80 DAYS

EUROPEAN PREMIERE

TUESDAY 22ND JUNE 2004

PRESS
PASS

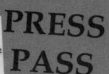

E: DAVE HOGAN

ORGANISATION:

PHOTOGRAPHE